GENRE

GENRE

A Guide to Writing for Stage and Screen

ANDREW TIDMARSH

B L O O M S B U R Y

LONDON · NEW DELHI · NEW YORK · SYDNEY

Bloomsbury Methuen Drama

An imprint of Bloomsbury Publishing Plc

50 Bedford Square	1385 Broadway
London	New York
WC1B 3DP	NY 10018
UK	USA

www.bloomsbury.com

Bloomsbury is a registered trade mark of Bloomsbury Publishing Plc

First published 2014

British Library Cataloguing-in-Publication Data
A catalogue record for this book is available from the British Library.

ISBN: PB: 978-1-4081-8582-7
ePDF: 978-1-4081-8493-6
ePub: 978-1-4725-3512-2

Library of Congress Cataloging-in-Publication Data
Tidmarsh, Andrew.
Genre: a guide to writing for stage and screen/by Andrew Tidmarsh.
pages cm
ISBN 978-1-4081-8582-7 (pbk.) – ISBN 978-1-4081-8493-6 (pdf ebook) – ISBN 978-1-4725-3512-2 (ebook)
1. Drama–Technique. 2. Playwriting. 3. Motion picture plays–Technique. 4. Screenwriting. I. Title.
PN1661.T53 2014
808.2'3–dc23
2013036186

Typeset by Deanta Global Publishing Services, Chennai, India
Printed and bound in India

For **Jacob**

(Just in case you need it one day)

Life isn't divided into genres. It's a horrifying, romantic, tragic, comical, science-fiction cowboy detective novel. You know, with a bit of pornography if you are lucky.

ALAN MOORE – *The Mustard Magazine (January 2005)*

www.mustardweb.org

The police are always off track with this shit! If they'd watch *Prom Night*, they'd save time! There's a formula to it. A very simple formula!

Scream

CONTENTS

ACKNOWLEDGEMENTS

In Memoriam: Syd Field 1935–2013

I would like to thank the following:

Dr Marion Gibbs and Professor Martin Dodsworth for igniting the spark all those years ago; John Ginman for asking me to teach a course on genre in the late nineties; Sophie Bradford for her help with the logistics; Conor Short, Cordelia Galloway and Emma Crates for being such encouraging readers of the early draft, pointing out some worrying errors and inconsistencies, and making such helpful suggestions; Karsten Schubert, Rosie and Dan for providing an inspiring place to write the final draft; Edward Kemp, James Thornton and Geoff Bullen at RADA; John O'Donovan (such a cheerful way of enforcing deadlines) and Jenny Ridout at Bloomsbury Methuen, and Sue Curnow for her eye for detail once again. A special thank you to Grishma Fredric.

My thanks also go to all my students over the years at Goldsmiths, Drama Centre and RADA. You have all contributed to this book.

INTRODUCTION

This book is intended to help make the blank page appear less terrifying.

We will be exploring the way different genres have evolved, and the way each type of story is embedded in a particular form. There will be exercises to help understand these forms. These exercises will hopefully ignite your creativity.

Whenever I teach genre, my students react with the enthusiasm of discovery: unity of time employed by Greek tragedians is still a device used to crank up the tension; the rules of Romantic Comedy have changed little, be it Shakespearean plays or contemporary Hollywood movies; the popular television series *Desperate Housewives* follows the pattern of Jacobean Tragedy almost exactly.

Students would rush into class gasping about a new connection that they had made:

– You know the comedy show *Friends*?
– Yes.
– It fits the rules for farce almost exactly!

No matter what the ages of the students were or what experience they had, the exploration into genre was always an adventure. Exploring the nature between form and content seems to bring endless discoveries and illuminations about how narrative works; how storytelling in film and theatre has evolved and how an appreciation of form can bring the writer, director or actor a solid foundation and a sense of security, which can sometimes surprisingly serve as a tremendous relief.

When you ask people to write a limerick, and explain the simple way the form functions, most people seem to be able to manage something:

She decided to cut her fair hair
While 3000 feet in the air.
The pilot went red
As he scornfully said
'Please wait 'til we land over there.'

It seems then that an awareness of form can assist the creative process. It can provide safety – the boundaries, rules and regulations that contain our creative impulses. The suggestion to write a poem produces anxiety and inactivity, but the suggestion to write a limerick – with its distinct form and rules – releases this creativity. Staring at a blank piece of paper produces inertia and procrastination; working out the words to fit five lines that rhyme in a specific way is an enjoyable challenge. The same is true of writing for the stage or screen. The idea of writing a play or screenplay seems like an impossibly huge task, but once we begin to reduce the infinite possibility of what that play might be, it becomes less overwhelming.

I suggest that all our stories require only one plot. Regardless of the genre, there is only one plot and all our stories are a variation of this single plot:

order → chaos → reorder

This is the story that we witness again and again, and this is the story that we tell over and over. An exploration of genre is to examine how this one story evolves into slightly different forms. We are going to explore the forms that support our storytelling on stage and screen, and this will hopefully release your creativity and inspire you to write, devise and tell your own stories. Understanding the functionality of form is the writer's craft.

This book is intended to help make the blank page appear less terrifying.

1
THE BUILDING BLOCKS
OF NARRATIVE

It seems strange perhaps that this field of enquiry has come about – whether in an academic context or in a more informal 'how to' context. Surely storytelling is a primary impulse, something that requires no analysis. It either works or it doesn't. Yet we dedicate time to discussing the mechanics of storytelling and analysing its efficacy. We turn to people like Syd Field[1] or Robert McKee,[2] looking for a usable formula. I remember telling stories to my young cousins without inhibition when I was a child, and paying no heed to the rules of story structure. They either remained interested or they didn't. I still question the use of some of the terms that we have come up with to build a story: 'inciting incident'; 'turning point'; 'reveal'; 'foil'; 'rising action'; 'story arcs'; 'character journeys'. Devising stories according to these terms robs them of all spontaneity and creativity. My initial advice regarding storytelling is tell the stories that you want to – the ones that interest you. This is the point where we will begin.

We will discuss the film *Tootsie* a great deal in the chapter on Romantic Comedy (Chapter 8). This film was in development for over four years, and they still hadn't finalized details about the story when it was time to shoot.[3] This length of time dedicated to a story's development is not an exception in writing films, plays or novels. So, why is so much time spent on devising, designing, structuring and rewriting?

The art of constructing a narrative might be seen quite simply. H. Porter Abbott explains that there are only two functions of narrative: to build suspense concerning what will happen next, or to reveal why something has already happened[4].

So, what makes a narrative compelling? If you have already read the introduction, then you will know the basis to the thesis on which this book is based: there is only one story – order turns into chaos, and then a new order arises from this chaos. Most stories fit this simple narrative structure. The mechanics of this narrative structure involve people making choices which then in turn bring about change. Change is central to this way of looking at narrative. Engaging stories are those in which relationships, attitudes, states are all in flux. That is it. It is that elementary. I am suggesting that there are two formulae on which all stories depend:

$$order \rightarrow chaos \rightarrow reorder$$

and

$$choice \rightarrow consequence \rightarrow change$$

However, the permutations and combinations that can be achieved around these two formulae are infinite. There are other important factors to keep in mind: logical cause and effect; recognisable relationships;

the handling of the exposition; the way information is revealed; transformation and the overall morality of the narrative.

A logical progression between cause and effect is important in building up trust in the audience. The narrative must have its own inherent integrity. The most clear illustration of a narrative not having integrity is seen in the way endings are wrapped up in many genres, but especially in thrillers and various television episodes in which a definite conclusion is needed. This involves the *deus ex machina* – something that both Horace and Aristotle warn against in their writings on poetic and narrative technique. As we encounter in *The Oresteia*, the gods descend to bring the narrative to a close, or as might happen in stories that are not ancient Greek or Roman, the hand of the author is clearly seen in bringing in new information to draw the story to a neat conclusion: the aliens catching a cold in *The War of the Worlds*[5]; the rucksack being left on the top of the Empire State Building at the end of *Sleepless in Seattle*[6] and the brother, David, changing his mind at the end of *Sabrina*.[7] The *deus ex machina* leaves the audience feeling somewhat cheated because their investment in the story has not paid off – the machinations of the author have become apparent, and the rules of the narrative have changed without warning or anticipation.

We often feel frustrated by thrillers, television crime series or episodes in which everything is hurried to reach a conclusion in under an hour, or in which the tension is sustained for the last possible moment for the resolve to happen suddenly at the end of the story. However this phenomenon is not only apparent when watching the way a story concludes; on any website which offers reviews, there will be comments and discussions about 'plot holes', instances when the author has not followed the logical development of cause and effect, and something has happened which seems at odds, a manipulation of the narrative. A coincidence, an erratic decision, an inauthentic response, an unlikely intuition are all examples of what might cause these possible holes in the plot. What would have happened in *Star Wars: Episode IV – A New Hope*[8] if Luke had not taken the right droids home? This would have been the case, were it not for a timely explosion in the droid that he first chose. In Shakespeare's *Othello*, what would have happened if the Turkish fleet had not sunk not long after Othello, Desdemona and Iago arrived on the island? The characters would have been too busy with war to trouble themselves with deceit and betrayal.

When causality is honoured, it appears as if the writer is rewarding the audience's attention with consistent and logical sequences of action, rather than plot holes or a *deus ex machina*. Perhaps this is something that makes a story successful or even durable; the hand of the writer seems almost invisible. When unity of action is involved, in Greek Tragedy for example, the process of events unfolding is condensed, and the consequentiality is robust. It is hard to locate the plot holes in *Oedipus, Antigone*[9] or *The Oresteia*.[10] Each event in the story seems to be a consequence of a character's previous action. Shakespeare, Chekhov and Ibsen have also produced durable stories. The characters seem so complete and autonomous in these dramas that when we are immersed in them, the hand of the writer is almost invisible. Hamlet's actions are often discussed as if he were a real person rather than a literary construction. The narrative in these cases is driven by characters' choices, and these choices are so considered and deliberate that the story appears to unfold organically.

There is relatively little work on character in this exploration of genre – a place where many practitioners and theorists advise writers to begin writing – working out who the characters are and what their individual histories might be. This is of course important work, but for our purposes we will be looking at the relationships between characters. According to the idea that narrative is driven by people making choices which then have consequences; the relationships between characters become more urgent and vibrant. It is almost as if, in this interpretation of narrative, the invisible space between people is more interesting than the people themselves. Hamlet is an interesting character, but it is his relationship with Claudius which drives the narrative: will he find the moral courage to kill the uncle whom he hates? Romeo and Juliet are appealing characters – young people on the threshold of adulthood – but it is the fact that they fall in love, and are forbidden from doing so, that drives the story. In addition, character is something fluid rather than something permanent; it is the relationships which cause the characters to change. It is Claudius' actions towards Hamlet that make Hamlet's final destruction of him an inevitability. Hamlet does not begin the play as someone able to commit a murder. It is the Capulets demanding Juliet's obedience which causes her to seek the Friar's advice and end up in the tomb waiting for Romeo. Perhaps a new way of thinking about story is required in order to construct an effective narrative: a move away from thinking about story as about character, and instead thinking about story as a web of evolving relationships. Making this shift means that characters are no longer set as something immutable. Instead they change as they interact with one another, and as we have seen, change is an essential element of storytelling. It is the ineffective narrative which is somehow static and stuck. This idea leads us again to the worlds of Ibsen and Chekhov. Their narratives generally involve characters freeing themselves from relationships in which they feel trapped and paralysed.

There is a skill in how writers handle exposition (or 'backstory' as some prefer). The audience need to know not only the world which the characters are inhabiting, but also who the characters are and how they are all connected. In short the audience need to know the 'rules of the game'. There is an obvious dilemma here. As well as giving all the necessary information to the audience, the narrative also needs to drive forward in order to keep the audience involved, and begin to build a degree of anticipation and suspense. It takes a very confident writer to stop the action in order to simply explain where we are and who everyone is; in fact it would take a writer as confident as Shakespeare was when he was already established as one of England's most celebrated dramatists.

Shakespeare is generally an expert in keeping the action moving forward while explaining the world and what has happened before the play begins – take the initial scenes in *Hamlet* or *Othello* as examples of this. In both, Shakespeare drives the action forward with excitement while at the same time pausing briefly now and again to have a character explain what is going on. However, in his later plays, he no longer seems to feel the need to fulfil both impulses at the same time; he has the action stop completely while he explains the 'backstory'. In the second scene of *The Tempest*, Prospero narrates the events that happened twelve years earlier to a sleepy and uninterested Miranda – events that are essential for the audience to understand if they are then to be engaged in the rest of the story. In *The Winter's Tale*, it is a simple conversation that explains the long history of Leontes, Hermione and Polyxenes, and introduces Leontes' sudden and overwhelming jealousy. However, most contemporary audiences are not used to remaining involved in such static narrative in which information is key, and in which the story does not seem to move forward.

As we know from action movies and television comedies, the narrative hook is one way of solving this tension: an opening scene which is so exciting or funny that we are immediately involved and committed to the story even though this initial episode has nothing to do with the subsequent narrative. James Bond films always begin this way, and so do episodes of the television comedy *Frasier*.[11] Each begins with an independent episode which is either comic or dramatic, the purpose of which is to grab our attention. Perhaps the most common way of handling the exposition is to have the audience share a point of entry into the story with one of the characters. Luke Skywalker in *Starwars: Episode IV – A New Hope* serves as our point of entry into the universe of Jedi knights and the clone wars. Certain comedies also seem to begin this way: both *Clueless*[12] and *Mean Girls*[13] begin with a new pupil being shown the school and the way the hierarchy there works. The arrival of a newcomer is also used in other comedies: Shakespeare's *Twelfth Night*, Wycherly's Restoration Comedy, *The Country Wife*[14], and *The Importance of Being Earnest*[15] by Oscar Wilde also depend on an arrival into the world featured in the play. The way this society functions is then explained to this newcomer. We, the audience, learn the rules of the world at the same time as the character who is actually involved in the story. There is a satisfying synchronicity between the character and the audience.

Even though the essential information is revealed at the beginning of the story, the way other information is revealed is part of the skill of the storyteller. As has already been suggested, we remain interested in story for one of two reasons – to see *what* will happen, or to see *why* something has happened. The *why* element, at its most evident, takes us into the realm of the thriller: the event has already happened, but will the detective find out who committed the murders and the reason the murderer did it? This becomes the basis of the suspense. All narrative contains some sort of secret in order for us to remain engaged. As the story of *Oedipus* progresses we are always asking both what will happen next and why did it happen. Our initial question is: will Oedipus succeed in lifting the curse on Thebes? The question then changes to: who killed Laius and why was he killed? Finally we ask: how did it come about that Oedipus killed his father without realising his crime, and what is he going to do now that he knows the awful truth? The initial suspense created by the question about what will happen next is sustained by the question about how the events came to be. The issue of *what* will happen is augmented by *how* it happened. Each new person who responds to Oedipus' summons brings with them a new piece of information. As each question is answered a new question arises.

This simple structure is perhaps plotting at its most effective, and satisfying stories contain this relationship between *what* and *how* regardless of genre. The comedy *Tootsie*[16] also mixes these questions of what and how. It begins with the question: what will Michael do to finally find employment and how does it come about that he dresses as Dorothy? We then ask two questions for the remainder of the film: How will those involved in the complicated love triangle (love square, actually) react when they discover that Dorothy is really a man, and how will Michael and Julie find love? These two questions create the suspense which keeps us asking what will happen next. The writers of *Tootsie* must choose exactly the moment when they reveal the information to the characters that Dorothy is really a man. However, there is no new information for the viewer to assimilate. We know information that the characters do not, and this dramatic irony is what is driving the comedy.

Often in contemporary film narrative, the important information is only revealed at the end. This is another form of *deus ex machina*, and as we have seen, when the hand of the writer becomes visible, the integrity of the narrative can be questioned. Rather than a sudden and unexpected action providing the resolve, as we saw with *Sabrina, War of the Worlds* and *Sleepless in Seattle*, a seemingly incongruous event occurs towards the end of the story which brings order to the events. There is almost a post-Freudian feel to the way some stories end: it is only by investigating the past and discovering the key that we can make sense of the present. The *Star Wars* trilogy of films (IV, V and VI) would be completely different films if we had known before Luke sets off on his adventure that Darth Vader is his father. Perhaps this is one of the reasons why parts I, II and III are less satisfying: we know *what* happens next (we know that Anakin becomes Darth), and on this occasion asking *how* it happens is less suspenseful.

Carefully choosing the moment to reveal an essential piece of information is a commonly used technique: both Chekhov and Ibsen use this technique in some of their stories; it is an essential technique for the thriller and the chivalric romance genres (as we will explore). It is telling perhaps that the stories of Shakespeare and those of Greek and Roman Tragedy rarely employ this structure. *Oedipus* and *Comedy of Errors* are two of the few examples in which a surprising reveal affects the outcome of the narrative. Otherwise, there are frequent reveals of information to the characters involved in the story, but generally the audience is already aware of all the important facts. For writers then, it is essential that information is revealed at a considered rate: the suspense must be maintained but the integrity of the narrative kept intact.

Peripety is a key factor in the way we are engaging with genre and looking at the structure of stories. Simply explained, this is the way something changes. The change will often involve a polemic shift: love might turn to hate, victory to defeat, companionship to abandonment, friendship to enmity, security to insecurity. When we are disappointed – either in the cinema or in the theatre – by ineffective storytelling, it is often simply because of not enough changes. The narrative seems slow, or static. Nothing happens. The story seems somehow stuck, and the characters seem stagnant and uninteresting. This, in my view, is sometimes a fault of a writing process that involves too much character work. It is important to know the information about the character – where they are from, what they do, whom they are related to – but the characteristics must be fluid: courage might turn to cowardice, honour to dishonour, generosity to selfishness.

We seem to be taught from quite a young age that all stories involve conflict. Conflict seems less important to me than change: all effective stories involve change. It is possible that change might be a result of a conflict, but it is change that keeps us involved and keeps us asking what will happen next. Perhaps a story involves only one substantial change: Oedipus changes from heroic investigator to pitiful perpetrator; Othello changes from loving husband to jealous murderer; Hamlet changes from procrastinator to man of action. There are no rules as to the frequency of the peripety. In Greek Tragedy we are generally dealing with only one transformation – that of the protagonist – and sometimes this change is as fundamental as from life to death: for example, Agamemnon, Antigone or Hecuba. Sometimes the nature of the change is more complex, as is the case with Oedipus. Sometimes the change happens to the universe rather than to the central character, as is the case in *The Orestia*. Different genres elicit different frequencies of peripety.

In Roman Tragedy and Jacobean Tragedy, there seems to be a change in every scene – sometimes gratuitously so, as a mechanism for keeping the audience engaged. Often in contemporary television drama there is a similar sense of peripety for the sake of audience engagement. Some television drama such as the US television series *90210*[17] is audacious in its use of peripety. Unexpected changes can happen in the space of one scene. It makes exciting drama, but we question the integrity of the writing. The effect of this is an inability to remember all the details of the plot. Similar to the element of causality, the integrity of the plot seems to hinge on the causal nature and frequency of the peripety.

Narrative contains an inherent morality within it, and this is reflected in the genre. Generally, our stories need to protect the innocent. Hence, the tragic hero brings about his or her own downfall, and anyone who inflicts suffering on the innocent is punished. To allow evil to flourish or to reward wrongdoing implies a lack of balance in the universe, and this is not something that belongs in our tradition of storytelling. One of the reasons stories are told is to reassure us that there is some order and purpose in our chaotic universe. In both tragedy and comedy we take a great deal of pleasure in the actions of characters who might be considered monsters, but these monsters ultimately experience some sort of downfall. The morality of the story is contained in how the story ends. This might seem like a redundant or old-fashioned idea, but it is central to the development of genre; each genre has its own inherent morality.

Jacobean Tragedy is distinct from Elizabethan Tragedy in terms of how the story ends and who is punished or rewarded and what state the world is in as a result of the action. A film by Quentin Tarantino has a different morality from that of a horror film in the *Saw*[18] franchise. Dr Frasier Crane is frequently punished for his pompousness; Larry David somehow manages to thrive despite his misanthropy.[19] However, morality is a more complex issue than the somewhat polarized matter of punishing the bad and rewarding the good. The stories that we are going to look at are frequently complex, and the characters embody both qualities at the same time; like all of us, their virtues exist alongside their flaws. Paolo Friere provides us with another way to measure the morality of narrative: are oppressed groups (or groups with a history of oppression) being given a chance to voice themselves or free themselves from oppression?[20] This is a complex issue, but it is one that we encounter daily when watching film, television or theatre: middle-aged women who are ridiculed for their sexual desires; criminals represented by gangs of black youths; gay men and women who always seem to lose; Hispanic characters in menial jobs who have no chance of improving their lives. Debates occur with regularity concerning these issues: why is any character from a minority demographic introduced to *Friends*[21] ultimately excluded from the all-white clique? Do films like *Bullet Boy*[22] and *Storm Damage*[23] reinforce an oppressive sensibility by portraying young black men who are given no chance of freeing themselves from crime and violence? 'Drip Theory' and 'Drench Theory'[24] give a clearer analysis of the morality of narrative, and how the portrayal of minority or peripheralised groups has an impact on the audience.

Causality, relationships, the exposition, reveals, choice and change, and the overall morality of the narrative are the building blocks of storytelling. This brings us to genre. We seem to enjoy having the same story told to us again and again. We take comfort in the repetition and enjoy our expectations being fulfilled. At the most basic level, we need to only look at many movie franchises. The *Bourne Identity* films are essentially the same story told over again: an agent who has lost his memory is hunted by his former department, must escape while at the same time finding a way to end the hunt. This is also true for the *Alien* franchise: a woman is trapped with a rageful and supremely destructive alien and for a time she is the only one who truly understands the nature of the danger while others wish to turn the alien into a weapon. Something might be added, details might change, but the story essentially remains the same. We are disappointed when there is a fundamental change to the story. *Alien 3*[25] is perhaps the least satisfying of the films, simply because unlike the others, there is a critical alteration to the form: Ripley dies at the end. Even when Sigourney Weaver and Matt Damon had left their respective film franchises, the series have continued without them: *The Bourne Legacy*[26] and *Prometheus*.[27] The story in each is a repetition of the original story in the sequence. It is easier to replace a main character than it is to change a critical element of the story. Analysis of these films is not meant to in any way criticize them or dismiss them. They are tremendously entertaining films which have been enjoyed by millions of people. Their popularity shows that we like to know what we are getting when we watch a film or a play. The power of repetition and expectation is great. Understanding genre is an extension of understanding how an *Alien* or *Bourne Identity* film works. Intellectual snobbery is futile.

All Shakespearean comedies essentially repeat the same story. All of Chekhov's plays essentially repeat the same story. All horror films or thrillers essentially repeat the same story. The locations, the contexts or the characters change, but the structure of the narrative remains the same. This immutable structure of each genre has come into being and endured because the storytelling is effective. The structures provide us with a way for our essential elements of story to fit together: causality, relationships, exposition, reveals and change. For a writer, understanding these structures brings rewards. The writer can concentrate on who the people are, and what the environment of the world is, while an understanding of the structure of the genre will take care of the mechanics of the plot. Understanding genre gives a form to support the writer's imagination. The blank page ceases to be intimidating as important elements of the story are already in place, waiting for the creativity and individuality of the writer to give the structure meaning.

There is only one plot: order moves to chaos then the chaos is brought to reorder. This plot has many forms. It is understanding these forms that makes writing and creating worlds exciting. The more that the writer understands these structures the greater the freedom that he or she has. The page is no longer a blank page waiting to be filled – infinite possibility has been reduced to a finite number of choices. As paradoxical as this seems, it is a liberating experience. It is exciting to discover that a story you are developing is improved by testing it against one of the prescribed frameworks of genre. Even though the essential elements of the stories remain the same, the possibilities are still inexhaustible, and as we will discover, once the framework has been understood, there is no reason why it cannot be altered or subverted.

Understanding genre is a way of being free from abstract narratology and of developing applicable tools instead. Notions of inciting incident, story arcs, rising and falling action become redundant. These abstractions are replaced with the structures of genre, and this in turn leads to effective, satisfying and fulfilling story.

2

WILL VERSUS FATE: GREEK TRAGEDY AND THE FUNDAMENTALS

By beginning with Greek Tragedy, we are not only beginning at the start of our Western tradition of narrative, but are also beginning with the genre that requires the most attention to shape or form. Examining how Greek Tragedy functions will give an insight into how adhering to a certain framework can actually assist the writer. This is the writer's craft: understanding the rules and regulations that the form demands, and how these demands can assist in the telling of a story. Writing or devising a piece of narrative inspired by Greek Tragedy requires the discipline to form a story according to a form which is over 2,000 years old. We have inherited this form not only from the plays that we have, but also from the descriptions of Aristotle[1]: the parameters are precise, and the rewards therefore are great. Examining this particular genre is a way of immediately immersing ourselves in the relationship between form and content.

The overriding appeal of Greek Tragedy is pertinent to both its form and its content: the journey of one protagonist from relative well-being to their downfall or their deaths. The qualities the tragic hero possesses, their story and the process which leads to their death (usually it is death, although there are some exceptions) are described in detail in Aristotle's *Poetics*. In many ways then much of the thinking has already been done for us several thousand years ago in ancient Greece.

In our somewhat sterilized and relatively safe society we are perhaps in the habit of forgetting the ubiquitous nature of death. This is one of the many functions of Greek Tragedy: it serves to allow us to practise the experience of grieving in a safe environment, and reminds us of our own mortality. If someone of high birth has to endure suffering and ultimately death, it might help us to put our own lives in perspective and perhaps be a little more prepared for the inevitable. Surprisingly, the worst factor about our inevitable end is not actually our own death. Our own individual deaths will be relatively easy; all we need do, hopefully, is surrender to the process, and hope that it is not too painful. Instead, the inevitable suffering in our lives involves being separated from those around us: our grandparents, our elderly relatives, our lovers, our friends, and, regretfully even our children. This is what drives the narrative of tragedy, a fear of separation, or even worse, abandonment. In these stories, parents are often separated from their children through the children's death. In *The Oresteia*,[2] Clytemnestra has lost Iphigenia; Jocasta has lost her son in *Oedipus*,[3] as well as Oedipus; Medea murders her own children[4] and Creon's son Haemon dies with Antigone in her tomb.[5] This seems to be a universal fear that we deal with in our storytelling. This is one story that forms a master plot: 'stories that connect with our deepest values, wishes and fears'.[6] It is the feelings that result from these separations, and the subsequent rage of abandonment that Greek Tragedy – indeed all tragedy – gives us an opportunity to experience and practise.

It is important that the tragic hero is someone of higher status than ourselves. If this is not the case, then the effect is not the same: we might be watching melodrama, kitchen-sink drama or even an ongoing television series. The distinction is that the people in these other dramas are clearly born into suffering and hardship. They do not appear to have a choice. They are victims of circumstance, and their situation is not necessarily a result of their own decisions and actions. Greek Tragedy reminds us that suffering is universal; even those of high birth experience suffering, but as we shall see, these figures seem to be given a choice, and their suffering is at some stage of the story often avoidable. As we will discover, this is a key point which defines Greek Tragedy.

Greek Tragedy is known for the three unities, the three dominant constraints which must be adhered to in the construction of the story.

Unity of Time

We seem unused to the stories that we watch happening in real time. Real requires the audience and the characters to be sharing the same timescale. Fifteen minutes of the audience's time, for example, is equal to fifteen minutes of the characters' time. There is no distinction between what Seymour Chapman refers to as the 'chrono-logic' of narrative.[7] Chrono-logic refers to the time span of the imaginary events of the story. There is an external movement through time – the duration of the film or play, and also an internal movement through time – the duration of the events that make up the story (for example, *The Winter's Tale* can be performed in about two and a half hours, but it covers a sequence of events that spans fifteen years). When unity of time is adhered to, these two schemes of time are the same. The chrono-logic corresponds to the running time.

There is a certain skill demanded of writers in sustaining the action and the story while keeping the events in real time. Our current cinematic and dramatic tastes produce stories that are broken up into short sections and often long periods of time pass between these sections of action – an hour, a week, several years. What is interesting is how easily the audience read these cuts in scene accurately. A contemporary audience seems to be able to follow the story effortlessly and understand what has happened in between the scenes. Our ability to understand sophisticated and disjointed time frames has become so acute that a film like *Blue Valentine*[8] can cut between two time streams without confusing its audience, and Christopher Nolan's *Memento*[9] has two strands, one of which runs forwards, and the other backwards. This complex use of time is also seen in some plays: Harold Pinter's *Betrayal*[10] runs backwards. However, his plays *The Homecoming*[11] or *The Caretaker*[12] adhere to a unity of time. There is something satisfying about linear narrative which moves forward in real time. It is something that is sometimes used in film-making although this form sometimes seems at odds with the film's natural advantage – the power of the cut: *Rope* (1948), *High Noon* (1952), *Fail Safe* (1964 and 2000), *Two Girls and a Guy* (1997) are all films that unfold in real time.

Although it may seem like a restriction, many writers actually find the idea of writing in real time a liberation. There is almost a relief in knowing that the story must be contained in the same time frame as the characters' understanding of time. Perhaps without the luxury of moving forwards or backwards in time, the events and nature of the story have to be planned out with care. There is more attention to causality. This awards the writer with a sense of their story being organic and in some way even wholesome.

Exercise – Writing in Real Time

This is a useful and challenging exercise. Writers are often surprised at how much can be learnt about story structure by doing this. Choose a length of time – perhaps begin with twenty or thirty minutes. Write a scene of this length which runs in real time. Only three characters may be involved, and you must include our simple structure for story: order leads to chaos, and this chaos evolves into a new order. Our second structure must also be included: someone has a choice to make, and the consequence of this choice is a major change. This structure will require your attention in several areas:

1   Entrances and exits: when characters enter and when they leave.

2   How action from 'off stage' is brought on and how it affects the story.

3   How the backstory is introduced at the same time as the action moves forward.

4   How suspense and interest is maintained: what will happen next? Or, how did it happen?

This simple exercise encourages the writer to engage with the mechanics of storytelling while exploring how scenes of dialogue function.

Unity of Place

This fits with one of theatre's most obvious conventions (or restrictions depending on how you view it); the stage represents one location only. This is a narrative constraint which appears to be at odds with a film's natural advantages – to change location frequently, and even pan between several locations. However, there are many films which do not change location, even though they do not necessarily adhere to unity of time: *Rear Window* (1954), *12 Angry Men* (1957), *The Breakfast Club* (1985), *Clerks* (1994) and *Blue in the Face* (1996).

There are many writers who consider that adhering to unity of place really tests their skill as storytellers. Like unity of time this can be strangely liberating and rewarding. To have all the details in place before writing starts has its benefits. The convergence of real time with one location can lead to writing that is measured, skilled and organic. Various narrative techniques will invariably accompany unity of time and unity of place: messages arriving, characters setting up exposition or revealing details of the past with storytelling, a misunderstanding, a death. These micro-narratives bring a new rhythm or energy to the story. They might lead to a change of direction or a change in a character's perspective. This is one of the ways that the story of Oedipus functions: although the play lasts only for a couple of hours, and is told in real time, the 'chrono-logic' of the story itself spans several decades. The micro-narratives of Tiresias or the shepherd contribute essential information which builds the narrative. In Greek Tragedy all the violence occurs off-stage; it happens in a different place or at a different time. This gives the unity of place an additional significance. The violent actions are always reported. Reported violence evolves into a significant element of the story-telling when we encounter it again in Roman Tragedy.

Exercise

Using micro-narratives and unity of place write a short play in which three people bring a story with them into the scene – something that happened earlier in the day, or even ten years ago. As each character reveals aspects of their micro-narrative, a larger narrative is formed. The two structures must be adhered to for the main narrative: order, chaos, reorder; and choice, consequence and change. This exercise will encourage you to explore how exposition (or backstory) can be employed, and how information is revealed to an audience. You do not need to adhere to unity of time if you do not wish. This structure is the basis of many plays. Its use is clearly effective in Conor McPherson's play, *The Weir*.[13] In Winsome Pinnock's play, *Mules*,[14] we are presented with a range of scenes concerning the chain in a drug-trafficking ring. Different worlds are presented to us, but she only ever writes for three characters on stage at the same time – as in Greek Tragedy. This is a highly effective form to tell this story. Only three actors are needed, but the narrative involves many more characters as the range of people making up the trafficking chain and their interconnectivity is explored.

Unity of Action

The simplest way of explaining unity of action is that there is no subplot or any other strands of narrative. All the action drives the sole plot forward, which, in the case of tragedy, takes us closer to the tragic hero's demise. There are no parallel plots running alongside the main plot, nor any digressions or diversions. There is no wastage in the construction of the narrative. H. Porter Abbot makes a distinction between *constituent events* and *supplementary events* in *The Cambridge Introduction to Narrative*.[15] *Constituent events* are necessary to drive the story forward and lead to other events. Even though *supplementary events* can be necessary in an overall understanding of the story, as they might provide extra details about a character or additions to the theme of the piece, they are not integral to the story. Keeping to *constituent events* and writing without digressions or diversions can test the integrity of the narrative and requires the plot to be constructed with skill. The causality of the narrative must be logical and consistent. This is not necessarily what we are used to. We seem to have become used to writing for television and film (and indeed theatre) in which multiple threads of action are divided up into short snappy scenes. Consider *Madmen*[16] or *The Sopranos*.[17] Often several threads of plot will weave together with different characters being involved in the different threads. It is often difficult to distinguish between what is a constituent event and what is a supplementary event. There sometimes seems to be a lack of economy in the writing as the audience is made to wait for action which contributes to the constituent event. These threads may then converge during the episode or even during the series.

Exercise

First write the scene, and then answer the questions that follow.

Write a scene which employs the three unities: time, place and action. The scene must last about twenty minutes and involve either two or three characters. No supplementary events may be included, but relevant exposition is allowed. This is to encourage you to explore the notion of economy. As in the previous exercises the structures of order, chaos, reorder and choice, consequence, and change must be employed.

Once you have written the scene, consider the following questions:

– What devices did you feel needed to be employed in order to sustain the action?

– How did you handle the exposition?

– What were your main challenges doing this exercise?

Exercise

Try writing dialogue which involves no exposition and no supplementary action. The characters engage only with the action in the moment. This is a counter-intuitive exercise for most writers. However, it can be instructive to be put in the situation of having to focus on driving the plot forward without digression. Do not be even tempted to explain who the characters are or where they are. This will become evident from the context as the scene progresses.

In Aristotle's *Poetics*, the tragic hero is described in detail, and he undertakes a specific journey. As has already been briefly mentioned, the person at the centre of the tragedy must be of a higher status than that of the audience. In addition, they must also be neither wholly morally good nor morally bad. It would seem that these two factors serve an important purpose: to provide distance from the character in the story, but at the same time to provide a degree of identification. The effect of the tragedy is not the same if the characters concerned are not either somehow aspirational to us or of higher status in some way. For example, compare how you feel when you experience the tragedy of Oedipus or Antigone with how you feel when you watch a gritty realistic drama set on a council estate, for example, *Nil by Mouth*,[18] *Ratcatcher*,[19] *Kes*[20] or *Shameless*.[21] A drama set in an environment to which we do not aspire does not have the same effect as that we experience when we watch Greek Tragedy. We experience perhaps a slightly voyeuristic impulse which then leaves us feeling despondent or hopeless that terrible things have happened to characters who are already unfortunate. This is not the effect of Greek Tragedy. The distinction is that when we watch the fall of someone greater or more important than ourselves, we feel almost lucky that this tragedy has escaped us, but at the same time wholly empathetic to the struggle of the main character because we are aware that the suffering has been brought about by a choice that the character has made, rather than a situation that they find themselves in. There is a distinction between these two different types of story, and their impact on the audience is different. We receive the story of a high-status person falling from grace differently from how we receive the story of a person in a recognisably everyday situation struggling to hope.

Catharsis is the name given to the experience of witnessing the fall of a tragic hero. When we have watched an effective tragedy, we feel somehow emotionally washed out. For the Greeks this was a sense of experiencing fear and pity. According to Aristotle, watching the suffering of the tragic hero can lead to the audience feeling exalted or even relieved. There is something pleasurable about watching the tragic hero's suffering.

The importance of the hero being neither wholly morally good nor wholly morally bad assists the audience in identifying with the character even though the character's high-status world is not immediately identifiable. The stories of Greek Tragedy do not concern the purely virtuous. These are not stories about the loss of innocence, or the preservation of innocence. These are stories about important people making choices, and these choices leading to their downfall. Often, essentially good people make poor choices: Oedipus, Creon and Phaedra, to name a few examples. It is not solely a matter of terrible things happening to characters in either a destitute environment or a prosperous setting. These are stories about high-status characters making choices that then lead to consequences. One of the structures that drive action in a story has already been introduced:

choice → consequence → change

This is the central pattern to a satisfying story. If we do not witness our protagonist making choices, but simply enduring terrible events happening to them, then the story is not fulfilling. We are simply watching the endurance of a character who is in the position of a victim.

This leads us neatly on to another element identified by Aristotle: *hamartia*. This is the error of judgement which leads to the main character's downfall. *Hamartia* is an essential element of the plot structure in Greek Tragedy. Our contemporary tastes perhaps involve stories in which the main characters react to unfortunate circumstances rather than take action themselves, and are therefore not fully responsible for the events which unfold. However in Greek Tragedy, it is always a choice and an act committed by the main character which give rise to the events in the story. For example, Oedipus persists in trying to release the people of Thebes from their plague, and in order to accomplish this he is to discover who was responsible for the murder of Laius. He is warned by Tiresias and others not to pursue the matter, but because of his tenacity (some might say arrogance), he discovers not only that he was responsible for the act of murder himself, but also that he has been living in an incestuous relationship with Jocasta, his mother, and his children have been the result of this incest. In the third play in the cycle, Antigone buries her brother, Polynices, against the commands of her uncle, Creon. This act then leads to her being buried alive in a tomb, and her subsequent suicide by hanging. Sometimes, *hamartia* is translated as 'fatal flaw'. It is my suggestion that we translate it as 'error in judgement'. For the writer or storyteller, this is a much more useful term, as the fundamental building block of narrative – 'choice, consequence and transformation' – is inherent in the term and this serves to remind us that a character's choice must be at the centre of their own demise.

The narrative is driven by one pivotal choice that the central character makes. The heroes in Greek Tragedy are not passive; they are not innocent bystanders who happen to get caught in external events. Through a specific choice, they inadvertently bring about their own downfall. In terms of the narrative, this choice then brings about a succession of events. It is motivated by the particular tension which seems to drive most of the stories in Greek Tragedy: *will* versus *fate*. It is the character's will that leads them to act despite the decree of fate that what they are doing is unwise or forbidden. In the case of Oedipus, fate is represented first by the Delphic Oracle which tells his father that he will be the victim of a patricide, then by the Delphic Oracle telling him how to lift the curse, and finally by Tiresias telling him to stop pursuing the matter. Oedipus believes that he can escape or subvert fate through willing it so. For Antigone, fate is represented by the higher authority of Creon who refuses to allow her to give her brother a fitting burial. The nature of the *hamartia* in these cases is *hubris*. When a character believes themselves to be untouchable, or almost god-like, this is *hubris*. It is sometimes translated as pride, but, actually, it is more than this, and for us *hubris* is something that sells newspapers and makes compelling reading. When we hear of some famous person's demise through their own error of judgement, *hubris* is sometimes involved. A drugs overdose, an infidelity discovered, unpaid taxes, an offensive comment made in public – all these events would suggest that the person considers themselves to be above the rules that govern the rest of us. Our reaction to the story is often mixed: we are fascinated by the event and the turnaround, but at the same time detached on some level – after all they only had themselves to blame. The element of *hamartia* has an additional benefit, as, if the story concerns a downfall brought about by the tragic hero's error of judgement, the causality is clear. The integrity of the story is kept intact as we are clearly able to follow the process of cause and effect, and the hand of the writer is less visible.

Sometimes a famous person involved in a scandal will give an interview that will then make us feel differently about them. We might develop a degree of sympathy, and understanding. In Greek Tragedy, this is called *anagnorisis*. At some point in the story, the tragic hero must take responsibility for their actions, and acknowledge that it is their choices that have brought about their downfall. The process is one of admitting responsibility. It is interesting that this concept is at the heart of many of the world's great religions: it is the notion of *tawbar* in Islam, the festival of *Yom Kippur* in Judaism, the Buddhist practice of repentance, and the sacrament of reconciliation (confession) in Christianity. Taking responsibility for what we have done also forms the basis of the Twelve Step Fellowship (Alcoholics Anonymous) and Freudian analysis. It would appear that there are tremendous benefits in anagnorisis: acceptance, healing, freedom from shame, hopefulness for the future. At the climax of the story, Oedipus acknowledges his responsibility for the curse on Thebes.

Another reason why we seem to be fascinated by the fall of a successful person – whether they might be fictional or factual – is that the turnaround is so great. This concept may be described in many different ways: a reversal of fortunes, a sea change, a polemic shift, a transition or a downfall. The Greeks referred to is as *peripitae*. It is a key element in storytelling. We will refer to it as 'peripety' throughout this book. According to Aristotle, the hero begins prosperous and well. Therefore, it is difficult to imagine a greater shift: from a position of power – respected, wealthy, secure – to death or abandonment. This is another reason why this genre is less suitable to everyday characters in a less glamorous context. If these stories are set among the poor or the already disenfranchised, the peripety which can occur is less dramatic; the height from which the tragic hero can fall is perceptively less.

Exercise

Consider the following points in order to structure a plot outline:

1   What environment do you consider to be inhabited by high-status characters?

2   Who is a person who lives or works in this context?

3   What is a choice that they might be forced to make involving fate versus will?

4   How might this choice bring about their downfall?

5   At what point do they realize that they are to blame for their own downfall?

6   What is the most dramatic peripety with which you can finish the story?

There is one more principle of Greek Tragedy that requires discussion: the closure (or ending) of the story. At the end of a Greek Tragedy, there is always a sense of hope, or that we are moving into a new order. This new order might simply be that everyone who has acted violently has now died, and there is a sense that the evil has been expunged and the world is now a better place having been somehow purged. This leads us to our essential narrative pattern. We have already discussed 'choice, consequence, change', and Greek Tragedy also adheres to the primary pattern for most storytelling:

$$order \rightarrow chaos \rightarrow reorder$$

In *Oedipus the King*, the source of the curse has been established, and Thebes is to be ruled by Creon alone. In the final play of the cycle, Antigone brings about Creon's own fall from grace, as he learns the consequences of pride. The cycle of evil begins many years before the action of the play: Jocasta and

Laius send their son to die in the wilderness in order to try and escape the predictions of the Oracle. This act of hubris is the first illustration of the tension between will and fate, and the story ultimately concludes with the destruction of a family and its lineage. The overall arc of the story sees the decline of a ruling family. The old order destroys itself and a new order is born.

Checklist

If you wish to base your narrative on the structure of a Greek Tragedy, here is a checklist:

- Death must in some way be involved. If the protagonist does not die, someone else connected to them does as a result of their actions or choice.

- The protagonist begins prosperous and well and finishes either dead or abandoned and destitute.

- The protagonist is of a higher status than the audience.

- The protagonist is confronted by a choice that needs to be made, and the result of this choice brings about the protagonist's downfall.

- The protagonist takes responsibility for the decision made and the resulting destruction.

- The choice in some way embodies the tension between will and fate.

- There is a sense of hope at the end of the story as a new order is established from the chaos.

- The three unities – time, place and action – are adhered to.

- The narrative is made of *constituent events*. There is an absence of supplementary events. The narrative is economic.

3
LET'S SEE BLOOD: ROMAN TRAGEDY AND QUENTIN TARANTINO

A violent society requires a violent narrative. Even though Roman Tragedy shares many of the same stories and characters as Greek Tragedy, the form is notably distinct. Similar stories, shaped differently, make a dramatically different impact. The other surprise when exploring this genre is how contemporary the plays of Seneca seem to us. They have a similar feel to them as contemporary film or television, and there are specific reasons for this. It is almost as if these plays have a similar sensibility to something written by Quentin Tarantino (*Pulp Fiction*,[1] *Reservoir Dogs*[2]) or Martin McDonagh (*The Pillowman*,[3] *In Bruges*[4]). They are also reminiscent of a television thriller, such as *The Killing*[5] or *The Fall*.[6] While there is violence in these plays, and the violence is extreme, it is not the violence that we associate with contemporary horror or 'slasher' movies such as those in the *Saw* or *Nightmare on Elm Street* franchises. There is often a pathos to the violence in Roman Tragedy which contextualizes it – giving it a weighty impact on the audience. When exposed to this type of violence we are moved, and overwhelmed with a sense of needless wastage.

Seneca (4 BC–AD 65) was a Roman philosopher, statesman, writer and dramatist. The story of his own life reads as though it might be material for one of his plays: exile, conspiracy, alleged murder plots and a violent and messy suicide. Whether his plays would have been performed or simply read is unclear. Abrams suggests that the plays were read, and that the English playwrights of the sixteenth century misunderstood how they were presented:

> Senecan tragedy was written to be recited rather than acted; but to the English playwrights, who thought that the tragedies had been intended for the stage, they provided the model for an organised five-act play with a complex plot and an elaborately formal style of dialogue.[7]

Regardless of the staging, the storytelling in the tragedies is compelling: fast-moving, urgent, moving and detailed. The plays teach us a great deal about constructing a narrative.

We will examine the differences between Greek and Roman Tragedy later in this chapter, but in brief, these are some of the clearest similarities and distinctions: the shape of the hero's journey remains true to Greek Tragedy; the unity of place is no longer applicable, while unity of time and unity of action still apply to some degree; the play is now divided into five separate acts (rather than five actions in a single act); there is less need for a new order to be defined at the end of the story; violence appears on stage as well as offstage, but the offstage violence is narrated with a precise degree of lengthy detail; the use of peripety is frequent; and there is no sense of a new order at the end of the story.

There seems to be less of an emphasis on the morality of the narrative in Roman Tragedy than there is in Greek Tragedy. There is a sense when we look at the stories that their main purpose is to excite and enthral an audience who is probably used to violence. The most startling innovation in Seneca's writing is the introduction of ghosts, the supernatural and madness into the narrative: in *Phaedra*[8] the plot is dependent on the sea monster that Theseus conjures up with Neptune's help, and in *The Trojan Women*,[9] the ghost of Achilles is urging the Greeks to complete their task, and sever the royal lineage of King Priam indefinitely before they depart from Troy. Even when we do not see the evidence of the supernatural directly, the details might be included in a micro-narrative: for example, in *The Trojan Women*, Andromache dreams of her dead husband urging her to save their son. This fascination with ghosts and ghost stories is, we assume, universal, reappearing in different forms in most cultures. The idea of something that does not belong on earth walking among us is appealing. The ghost might bring with it a message from the 'other side', or it might be appearing because it has unfinished business on earth. The implication is usually the same – something is not right in the world as the natural order is inverted: death is not followed by eternal peace, but by restless nocturnal wandering. Regardless of the genre, the appearance of a ghost is usually accompanied by a sense of something being amiss, and the need for some sort of reconciliation. Ghosts walk the earth because they are literally unable to rest in peace. In *Apocolycyntosis*,[10] his satirical work about the Emperor Claudius, Seneca claims that ghosts may be the souls of those who died prematurely or violently or both.

Like ghosts, madness is also a sign that there is something wrong, that the natural order has in some way been upset. Madness in stories is a sign that a character is no longer coping. The character is rejecting reality in favour of an inner fantasy. This might be because they are overwhelmed, and are no longer able to contain the emotions that reality demands of them. So an escape into an incoherent fantasy world is preferable. It is a sign that the person has in some way broken. Racked with guilt, remorse and sorrow, Phaedra can no longer cope with her involvement in Hippolytus' death and so speaks to his remains as if he were still alive, before stabbing herself so that she might join him. The story of *The Trojan Women* is framed by Hecuba questioning how she might be able to contain so much suffering:

> A young child and an innocent girl have died;
> The war is over. Where shall I now weep?
> Where will they let my aged mouth spit out this lingering
> Taste of death? Daughter, or grandson,
> Husband, or country – which desires my tears?[11]

Hecuba is just able to contain these feelings of grief. She would like death to relieve her of her suffering, but unlike other characters in Seneca's plays, she is still sane. Hecuba's speech gives us an indication of the heightened emotions that are involved in these dramas, and how madness might be a possible escape from looking for reason in such terrible circumstances.

These are themes that fascinate us still. Consider the popularity of such films as *Sixth Sense* (1999), *The Others* (2001) and *The Orphanage* (2007). The world of the living and the world of the dead coexist in each of these films, and there is also the implication that trauma has occurred, and that a character is no longer perceiving the world entirely rationally.

Exercise

Consider a ghost story, and write a plot outline. What is the cause of the ghost's appearance? Who has the ghost chosen to appear to? Is there a matter which requires resolve? If so, how?

Once you have written a plot outline, consider the following. What specific tone is established once the ghost is introduced? What emotional turmoil do the characters experience once the ghost appears? Does anyone question the reality of this, or indeed of their sanity?

Another development from Greek Tragedy initiated by Seneca is the introduction of onstage violence. As we have already seen, Phaedra stabs herself in a fit of passion, when confronted by the body of Hippolytus. In *The Trojan Women*, we witness Andromache tear her hair out in her husband's tomb, as she betrays her son, Astyanax, and hands him over to Ulysses for sacrifice. We know from contemporary theatre, or from the experience of watching a film at the cinema, the impact that a sudden act of violence has on an audience. The collective gasp serves as a punctuation of the story and is symptomatic of the enjoyable feeling of inclusion that the audience feel despite the shocking events. In addition to onstage violence, Seneca develops the violence that is reported by adding meticulous detail to the narration. The reporting of the offstage violence in Roman Tragedy is rich. The narrator explains the extent of the violence with a meticulous detail. Hippolytus's death in *Phaedra* is described by the messenger with a precision that is both repulsive and thrilling. We hear how his pelvis is impaled, how his body is ripped apart by the fleeing horses and how his brain is scattered through the rocky landscape.

> Now half dead
> His flesh is ripped by brambles, gored by spines
> Of thorny thickets, broken into pieces
> Hanging on every tree. And sadly now
> His servants and companions search the ground
> Wherever the long trail of blood marks out
> The passage of the torn and dragged Hippolytus[12]

The violent scene of the body being ripped apart is vivid, and we are transfixed by the repetitious gore and horror. The detailed violence in *The Trojan Women* takes on a different tone. These reports tell of the murders of the two children Astyanax and Polyxena. While the deaths are told with close attention to detail, reported also is the reaction to the violence and the ironic regret of the Greek men who have initiated the execution, as they stand and watch with tears in their eyes. The sacrifice of Polyxena is made even more brutal by the humiliation she must endure before she is killed; she is dressed as a bride, and led in a wedding procession to be married to the dead Achilles before she is sacrificed.

The detail in both these narrations serves a distinct purpose. Not only does it provide illustration and detail, but by delaying the action of the narrative to paint such lucid pictures, suspense is created as we wait for the inevitable death. Delaying the action by speech making, and thereby creating suspense, is a technique that Seneca often exploits. This anticipation ends with the reward of excessive and graphic descriptions of smashed bones, scattered brains and spurting blood. It is this combination of suspense and detail that makes the devastation, and sense of waste so complete. This technique – even when it is narrated – is surprisingly film like. Time is taken to explore the nature of violence. This may be narrated in Roman Tragedy, rather than shown, as it is in film, but there is still a fascination with the detail of violence and a need to get as close to it as possible.

When there is a sporting victory (or defeat), it is replayed over again, from different angles and even slowed down so that we may absorb every nuance of the moment. The way Seneca dissects dramatic moments with such attention to the violent detail is the ancient Roman equivalent of this playback. Our shock and trauma at the extent of the horror and mutilation is given space, so we have the opportunity to enjoy the moment fully. Quentin Tarantino's *Pulp Fiction*[13] uses narrated action in a similar way to Seneca. Our fear of Mr Wallace is built up through a story about him throwing someone out of a window for massaging his wife's feet, and the story of the watch being brought home from Vietnam is told with a meticulous eye for detail by Captain Koons to the young Butch Coolidge.

Exercise

Write a scene in which one character narrates a story of terrible violence with meticulous detail. What is the effect on the other characters? How do they respond? How do you sustain suspense while having a character narrate for such a long time?

Exercise

Write a scene in which a narrated event is used to delay the action, and thereby create a heightened degree of suspense.

The sense of devastation which we feel from this violence is then accentuated by the fact that there is no reordering. In Greek Tragedy, there is a sense that the world has become a better place because of the violence and loss. However, in Roman Tragedy, this is not the case. Rather than adhering to the basic structure of *order → chaos → reorder*, we are left with *order → chaos →* and then *remorse*. This gives us the impression that Seneca's stories are personal and intimate stories. There is no additional public layer of the story, no sense of the community evolving after the horrors of the tragedy. The wider world of the state is not represented in the context of the play; instead the impact of the events is entirely from a personal point of view. This sensibility seems current. It is the sensibility of the contemporary Hollywood film. Let us take *Pulp Fiction*, again, as an example. Even though the film opens with a conversation about hamburgers in Paris, this is one of the only glimpses that we get of a world outside the film. Another glimpse of something outside the story is when Bruce Willis's character, Butch, successfully escapes the world of violence, and we sense that his exit from this environment is also his redemption. Apart from these few moments, the characters are mainly inward looking. They are wholly involved in the violence that they create, and there is a sense that this violence is gratuitous – a result of the choices that the characters are making, and ultimately these choices could have been avoided. It is a strange catharsis that we experience. Unlike in Greek Tragedy, we feel fear and pity, but we do not feel in some way purged and cleansed. We feel somehow sullied or distressed and need some time to recover.

In Greek Tragedy, the central tension is *will* versus *fate*. This is not the case in Roman Tragedy, where the central choice that the tragic hero makes, which then leads to their downfall, is driven by *head* versus *heart*. Phaedra knows that her love for Hippolytus is wrong. Her heart wills it even though her head knows how wrong it is to fall in love with her own stepson. In other words the central tension is *reason* versus *passion*, or *intellect* versus *impulse*. In *The Trojan Women*, there are several examples of this: Andromache deciding whether to give up Astyanax; the Greeks' reaction to the deaths of the young Trojans; Hecuba's response to the events of the play. This provides us with another reason why the plays of Seneca appear so contemporary. Our current stories often revolve around this tension, and it appeals in a range of plays and films: vampire stories; romantic comedies; stories of superheroes; medical dramas or family dramas. All these different types of story may well involve a decision that needs to be made between head and heart. Perhaps we are so drawn to this particular tension because the memorable and difficult decisions that we ourselves make in life are similar: whether to accept a particular job; whether to begin (or end) a relationship or love affair; whether to commit to a relationship or whether to accept an advantageous offer despite our moral scruples. Our model of choice → consequence → change also holds true for Roman Tragedy. It is the act of watching the character making the choice that is part of the fascination of the story.

Owing to the forensic rhetoric which Seneca employs, the moment of choice is delayed and the suspense is increased. Forensic rhetoric is a device also employed by the Elizabethan writers to explore moments of choice. It involves a speech which embodies the decision-making process. It is only by speaking that the character makes up his or her mind. The characters genuinely do not know what they are going to do before they start speaking.

Exercise

Part 1

Consider a situation in which a choice must be made. The choice involves the tension between head and heart. Suspend your character in the moment of indecision, and have them talk through the decision. Remember, they do not know what they will decide before they start speaking. The stakes must be high: life, death, abandonment, or betrayal.

Part 2

Just at the point when the character believes that they have made a choice, introduce a new piece of information that changes the head/heart choice that needs to be made.

Seneca employed a specific technique, *stichomythia*, to show someone trying to negotiate this choice. This involved characters who represent different points of view having a discussion or argument about the issue at hand. However, the dialogue proceeds with each character speaking only one short line, or even half a line.

> **Nurse:** He'll run from you –
> **Phaedra:** – run, even from the sea, I'll follow still.
> **Nurse:** Do you forget your father?
> **Phaedra:** No, nor my mother.
> **Nurse:** But he hates all women.
> **Phaedra:** The less I'll fear a rival.[14]

The same technique is used in *The Trojan Women* when Agamemnon and Pyrrhus debate whether to sacrifice the young Trojans. Ulysses debating the giving up of Astyanax with Andromache also involves these short lines and quick exchanges of stichomythia.

Exercise

Return to the scenarios of the previous exercise. Choose an appropriate moment when the choice that the protagonist must make is clear. Write some dialogue which explores this moment. To begin with write normal dialogue in which you do not pay too much attention to the length of lines. Once the scene has been established, write the dialogue according to the form of stichomythia.

Now answer these questions:

–   How does the stichomythia change the tone of the scene?

–   What does this form of dialogue add to the scene?

–   How does this form of dialogue contribute to the storytelling?

–   Would you consider it a useful technique to employ in your own writing?

Checklist

Here is a checklist if you wish to base your writing on the model of Senecan Tragedy:

•   The Aristotelian model for the tragic hero is still applicable, including hamartia (an error of judgement) and anagnorisis (acceptance of responsibility).

•   There is now a five-act structure, each act containing a definite element of the action.

•   Madness, onstage violence and the supernatural are all elements of the story.

•   The main tension is one of head versus heart, or intellect versus feeling.

•   Suspend the tragic hero in a moment of choice, and use forensic rhetoric and stichomythia.

•   Offstage violence is narrated with meticulous attention to detail.

•   Peripety is a feature of most scenes.

•   There is no need for reordering.

•   The story begins with a sense of impending doom, before anything happens.

•   This is not a story about evil. It is a story about someone making a wrong choice.

4
REVENGE IS SWEET: ELIZABETHAN TRAGEDY

The Spanish Tragedy[1] involves a father's elaborate revenge for the death of his son. The story involves nine deaths, two people going mad and someone biting out their own tongue. The events unfold under the watchful gaze of the spirit of Revenge. Shakespeare's *Hamlet* is a play which involves one man making a very difficult choice. Unusually, the play involves the consequences of not making a choice, or rather choosing to procrastinate rather than take action. The choice that Hamlet must make concerns killing his uncle as an act of revenge for killing his father. Hamlet considers the moral implications of taking this act of revenge, and this is one of the reasons that he does not act immediately. These are heightened dramas exploring extreme situations and demanding that the characters make some difficult choices which lead to violent consequences.

The fascination with Revenge Tragedy is perhaps because of the fact that revenge has always been (and is still) a delicious taboo. An act of revenge epitomizes the tension that we discussed when looking at Roman Tragedy, that of head versus heart. We know that revenge is wrong intellectually, and that it is forbidden within a religious context:

> For we know him that hath said, Vengeance belongeth unto me, I will recompense saith the Lord. And again the Lord shall judge his people.
>
> Hebrews 10

and also:

> But I say unto you, that you resist not evil: but whosoever shall smite thee on thy right cheek, turn to him the other also.
>
> Matthew 5

This is the basis on which our society is built. It is up to the law to seek retribution, not us as individuals. A civilized culture is based on justice being preferable to vengeance. However, despite the fact that we know revenge is wrong, we often still desire it, or even demand it. Prison dramas, gangster stories, thrillers and some horror films depend on the thirst for revenge. For our purposes, Elizabethan Revenge Tragedy is appealing because of the way tragedy further evolves. It is a fascinating hybrid of Greek and Roman Tragedy, adhering to some of the values of these genres while flaunting others. *In the Bedroom*,[2] *Get Carter*,[3] *Oldboy*,[4] *Straw Dogs*,[5] *Cape Fear*[6] are all films that involve revenge in some way. Interestingly three of these films have had fairly recent remakes. This is an indication of the effective and enduring nature of stories that involve revenge.

Arguably, the point of this is to help us to examine our morality. There are some basic assumptions that we might make about moral duty. I imagine we all hope that at the heart of all civilized belief-systems is the notion that it is the duty of the strong to protect the weak or of the powerful to protect the powerless. Perhaps this is not actually the case, but it is an ideal we might aspire to. Innocence is something that ought to be preserved. We imagine that this is the mark of a civilized society – the vulnerable are not open to exploitation. This is not the case in this mode of storytelling. In Elizabethan Revenge Tragedy, the powerless are often exploited, the innocent corrupted and the weak destroyed by the strong. These are the stories that give us two definite elements to engage with: the vicarious pleasure of watching illicit justice being violently carried out, while at the same time engaging with our epistemic duty – our duty not only to do the right thing, but also to seek out the truth and examine our systems of morality and question what is right and what is wrong.

Revenge Tragedy certainly subscribes to our fundamental model for narrative structure:

$$\text{order} \rightarrow \text{chaos} \rightarrow \text{reorder}$$

Elizabethan Revenge Tragedy adheres to this pattern on two levels: the personal and the public. On the personal level the tragic hero experiences a descent into chaos as, following a sudden and shocking murder, their inner belief system no longer matches with the newly formed perception of an unjust outer world. This is certainly true in the case of *Hamlet*, and the nature of Hamlet's procrastination perhaps concerns his inability to reconcile his inner beliefs with his outer perception as he comes to terms with the realisation that his world is not what he once thought it was:

How weary, stale, flat and unprofitable
Seem to me all the uses of this world.[7]

Likewise, the public world is also descending into chaos in *Hamlet*. There has been a murder, and a usurpation. The Danish court is no longer one of action and war, as it was when old Hamlet was king, but it is now guided by Claudius's new values – his talent for diplomacy. These changes seem all the more awkward by the way that the king has changed but the queen has remained the same, as the queen has now married her brother-in-law. Clearly, this is a court and a country experiencing the chaos that accompanies any transition. We are told that 'something is rotten' in the state of Denmark, and that the time is 'out or joint'. Through a sequence of murders caused by attempts at revenge, reorder on a public level will be established by the end of the play. Like a Greek or Roman Tragedy, everyone who is somehow touched by the evil which initiated the events will be dead. Denmark will once again become stable. As is the case in Greek Tragedy, the new order that is established means that the audience leave with their sadness at the tragedy tinged with a feeling of hope. The corruption and expediency has been expunged, and a new order will bring a better future. All those who have somehow been involved in the acts of evil or violence – including the tragic hero who has perpetrated an act of revenge – are dead.

Exercise

Consider a plot for a Revenge Tragedy in a contemporary setting. As with Greek Tragedy, a high-status main character is advisable. Consider the choices that the characters are faced with, and how a new order is established out of the chaos of an initial murder. How will your story challenge the audience's own morality and make them question the notions of right and wrong?

The journey that the hero undertakes is similar to that of the tragic hero in Greek Tragedy. Aristotle's description of the tragic hero is still applicable, and the conventions that he noted are adhered to. The hero begins prosperous and well, and it is ultimately through an error of judgement (hamartia) that his or her own downfall is brought about. Like in Greek Tragedy, there will be a moment of recognition (anagnorisis), as the hero acknowledges that they must take responsibility for their downturn in fortune. This process of taking responsibility is important, as we discussed when looking at Greek Tragedy, as it somehow serves to keep the tragic hero sympathetic to the audience. They are reconciled to their fate, and to their part in bringing these events about. They remain somehow noble and dignified, and worthy of our interest and attention. This redemption is something that we are quite used to in stories. Sometimes the error of judgement concerns arrogance or pride, and the arrogant main character is redeemed by seeing his hubris for what it is and learning humility. This narrative trope is widespread regardless of genre: Scrooge in *A Christmas Carol*,[8] Jack Nicholson's characters in the comedies *As Good as it Gets*[9] and *About Schmidt*.[10] It would appear that comeuppance and redemption are an archetypal story.

Our second narrative structure is equally valid for Revenge Tragedy. While the overall structure might be one of reorder following chaos, the process that provides the impulse to the story is

$$\text{choice} \rightarrow \text{consequence} \rightarrow \text{change}$$

As we have preciously explored, this sequence is central to all effective storytelling. Without it the audience's commitment to the story is minimal. Causality is essential in our narratives. A character behaves in a certain way because of a particular impulse and a choice that arises, and this leads to a particular consequence and something changes. Stories that do not adhere to this pattern can lead to an impression that they are perhaps concept-driven rather than narrative-driven: plays by Beckett or Satre, films such as *Inception* (2010), or *A Single Man* (2009). In these cases the presence of the playwright, screenwriter or film-maker is felt, and the audience defer somewhat to their control and superiority, rather than allowing an organic structure of unfolding events to be witnessed.

Aristotle suggests an organic structure for tragedy, and this is served by causality. There is another layer to this, however. We seem to be fascinated by watching people making choices. Light television entertainment thrives on this: many choices leading to dramatic consequences keeps the action exciting. In Revenge Tragedy, there is a moment when the protagonist makes the decision to take the action upon himself and commit murder:

> But wherefore waste I mine unfruitful words,
> When nought but blood will satisfy my woes?
> I will go plain me to my lord the king,
> And cry aloud for justice through the court,
> Wearing the flints with these my withered feet,
> And either purchase justice by entreats,
> Or tire them all with my revenging threats.
>
> *The Spanish Tragedy*, Act III, Scene viii

As we can see, this decision is unsurprisingly accompanied by heightened emotion: anger, rage, despair, self-loathing, regret. The tradition of Revenge Tragedy illuminates and explores the complexity of feelings that lead to a rational person making the decision to kill.

Exercise

Write a scene in which someone explains the decision they have made to end someone else's life. Decide on the context. Is it before or after the killing? How sure are they that they are going to do it? What is the context that has led to the decision? How much of the detail are you going to reveal to the audience at this point?

The challenge when writing this scene is to make your protagonist as honest as possible; sympathy and understanding are the result of this honesty.

Seen in this context, *Hamlet* is an even more fascinating play. Shakespeare has created a situation in which vengeance is required, and the protagonist is unable to make up his mind.

> Thus conscience does make cowards of us all,
> And thus the native hue of resolution
> Is sicklied o'er with the pale cast of thought;
> And enterprises of great pith and moment,
> With this regard, their currents turn awry,
> And lose the name of action.[11]

This is what makes *Hamlet* so compelling. It is a play in which the main character is trapped between head and heart, intuition and intellect. Unable to solve this conundrum, he becomes involved in thoughts, strategies, excuses and schemes which further distract him from his one objective – to kill his uncle. Throughout this process, he experiences many complex emotions, including rage, denial, confusion, disempowerment and despair. Shakespeare is examining a man who is stuck: he is trying to make a choice – our expectation, according to the genre, is that he will make up his mind swiftly after a short period of consideration. But Shakespeare subverts our expectation. When Hamlet finally decides to kill Claudius, it is too late – Claudius has set a plan in motion to have Hamlet killed. Hamlet's delay is part of his hamartia; his error of judgement is his inability to commit to a decision, and Hamlet (at his moment of anagnorisis) takes responsibility for this.

As we can see with *Hamlet*, Elizabethan Revenge Tragedy develops the Aristotelian conventions of the protagonist's process including the use of hamartia, anagnorisis and hubris. It also adheres to many of the Roman conventions of tragedy: the use of the supernatural, the presence of madness and graphic onstage violence. These elements clearly add to the action in the two revenge tragedies that we are exploring. In the *Spanish Tragedy*, the murdered officer, Andrea is onstage throughout the play, and the spirit of Revenge reassures him throughout that those who are responsible for his death will get their comeuppance. *Hamlet* also begins with a ghost: the appearance of the old king to the watchmen. This inclusion of something other than the earthly and other than the heavenly gives the plays a distinct tone. The parade of the dead that we witness in *Richard III* or *Macbeth* is reminiscent of the appearance of ghosts in the Roman tragedies of Seneca. An Elizabethan audience would have understood that with this supernatural content, they are to watch something tempting and alluring, but also immoral, perhaps even illicit according to their world view. The fact that the supernatural element concerns someone who has been murdered adds to the appeal. The audience's interest is immediately piqued by the sensational presence of the supernatural. In these cases it serves as a narrative hook. If we consider the enduring appeal of novels like *The Turn of the Screw* or *The Woman in Black* (also a long-running West End stage play, and a film), or films like *The Sixth Sense* (1999) or *The Others* (2001), then it is clear that – like an Elizabethan audience – we still find tales of the supernatural fascinating.

The inclusion of madness further develops the tone that is established by the supernatural element, and the inclusion of it entices the audience even more with something that is titillating, fascinating and almost a forbidden pleasure. The appeal of madness is that, like the supernatural, it suggests something 'other'. A character has detached from reality, and they are no longer behaving in a way that is rational or reasonable. The madness might be inspired by the schism caused by inner belief and outer perception, and the rage that this provokes. This certainly seems to be the case with both Hamlet and Hieronimo (Hieronimo from *The Spanish Tragedy*). Their madness is provoked by the need to act in a way that they would previously have thought uncivilized. They were once rational people, and they are coming to terms with the new idea that they have to behave in a way that they would once have considered immoral, or even animal. The other literary archetype which involves madness is that of the woman who has somehow been wronged. The suggestion is that their suffering then perhaps gives them a deeper insight into the workings of the universe, and this clarity of vision, or trauma, cannot be contained within the framework of rational perception, and so rationality is forfeited. This certainly appears to be the case with Cassandra (*The Trojan Women*), Ophelia (*Hamlet*), Lady Macbeth (*Macbeth*) and The Gaoler's Daughter (*Two Noble Kinsmen*). Arguably Blanche Dubois (*A Streetcar Named Desire*) is a descendant of this literary figure. However, this type of insanity soon evolves into something else in Jacobean Tragedy, and then again into something else in the Victorian Novel (*Jane Eyre*, *The Woman in White*).[12] It would appear that each period reinvents the figure of the woman afflicted with insanity for their own purposes.

In terms of narrative structure, the use of madness and ghosts serves to build suspense. If we acknowledge the significance of two of the principles that drive narrative forward – expectation (the proairetic code) and questions and answers (the hermeneutic code)[13] – then we can see how useful supernatural elements and madness are in contributing to the story. Both elements challenge our normal expectation as we are taken into a less rational world, one in which we anticipate the next appearance of the supernatural (proairectic) and we are left asking questions (hermeneutic). Why has he or she gone mad? Why is a ghost appearing? Is the ghost really there? A world which contains the supernatural, and insanity is a world in which causality is no longer an essential factor; anything can happen at any time. Both writer and audience are liberated from the usual constraints of cause and effect. This is an exciting world in which a narrative can be set.

Exercise

Consider an idea for a ghost story. When is the most unexpected time for the ghost to appear? Can everyone see the ghost, or just one character? What is the nature of the trauma that has caused the ghost?

By the end of the story certain questions must be answered: Who is the ghost? Why is he or she appearing? What do they want?

Elizabethan revenge drama introduces meta-textual elements into storytelling. There is often a play within a play. In *The Spanish Tragedy*, the performance is used by Hieronimo to perform the murders and carry out the necessary revenge. In *Hamlet*, it is the play within the play, the 'mouse trap' which convinces Hamlet of Claudius's guilt. It would seem that each generation reinvents meta-textuality for itself, and experiments with narrative which in some way expresses a self-conscious awareness of its own form: characters coming on stage from the audience in Beaumont's seventeenth-century comedy, *Knight of the Burning Pestle*;[14] Pirandello's early twentieth-century play, *Six Characters in Search of an Author*,[15] Brecht's use of a play within a play in *The Caucasian Chalk Circle*;[16] characters in *The Sopranos* watching and doing impressions and watching their favourite parts from *The Godfather* films; Larry David reuniting the cast of *Seinfeld* in *Curb your Enthusiasm*. The use is widespread and the nature of its usage varies. As these examples show, it is not a device limited to Revenge Tragedy.

In Elizabethan theatre there was no way of focusing light. Essentially, the audience shared the same light as that of the actors. This is true for theatres such as the Globe and the Rose, where the performance would have been at two o'clock in the afternoon, and it is also true for indoor spaces such as Middle Temple Hall where the room would have been lit by candlelight. Perhaps the meta-textuality, then, is a result of this theatrical necessity. The Elizabethans are likely to put people watching plays into their dramas because that very activity is so apparent during the performance all around them. In a way the Elizabethan theatre has a freedom that the notion of realism has yet to restrict. Realism and naturalism can be quite prohibitive in some ways. If everything on stage (or in a film) has to sustain the illusion of reality, the effort involved in upholding the illusion of realism can be overwhelming and dominate the aesthetic and the values of the finished project. The Elizabethans had no convention of the fourth wall. Characters may come out of the action and talk directly to their audience because there is no attempt to conceal the fact that audience and actors are sharing the same experience and space. The soliloquy, then, is a part of this meta-textual tradition. A character can divulge their inner thoughts or comment on the action by simply addressing the audience. Within the conventions of realism, a dialogue needs to be contrived in order for a character to reveal what they are thinking. Perhaps this is why Batman needs Robin.

To have moments in a narrative when the audience and actors become self-consciously aware of the form that they are inhabiting has a surprising effect. This effect is twofold. Initially, the audience is jolted from the illusion and the suspension of their disbelief, as they become aware of the fact that they are sitting in a theatre or a cinema, experiencing an audience on stage (or on screen) in the same position as they are in. Like Russian 'nesting' dolls, the narrative develops layers of one audience watching another audience watching. Often, however, this is followed by a secondary impulse: to become more involved in the narrative than before. The honest statement of awareness within the narrative that it is a work of fiction gives the audience a choice – they can either accept or reject the narrative. Once given this choice we often decide to commit to the narrative with a new degree of intensity, aware that it is a play or a film. The effects of meta-textuality perhaps are the opposite of what we might expect. Because we experience a play within a play, or a film within a film, we disregard the artifice and illusion more eagerly, and accept more readily the reality offered by the narrative.

Like Roman Tragedy, forensic rhetoric is a feature of Elizabethan Revenge Tragedy when making a speech directly to the audience. A character has a choice to make, and genuinely does not know what he or she is going to decide until the speech is finished. Speaking to the audience becomes part of the decision-making process.

Exercise

In both *Hamlet* and *The Spanish Tragedy*, the play within a play is essential to the narrative development. Write a scene in which the watching of a play or a film initiates the narrative impulse of 'choice – consequence – change'. So, the meta-textual element drives the narrative, rather than it simply informing the narrative thematically.

We have discussed the central tension which drives both Greek Tragedy (will versus fate) and Roman Tragedy (head versus heart). The central tension which drives the narrative in Elizabethan Revenge Tragedy relates to our initial discussion on revenge. Once the act of revenge is committed the protagonist has fallen. He or she is now no better than the person they want vengeance on; they have committed the same crime or sin, and the cycle of revenge will then perpetuate itself until it stops, and – as in Greek Tragedy – we are left with the question: where does evil end? Elizabethan Revenge Tragedy asks an additional question: What is it that makes us human and distinct from the animals? When thinking about his mother's sudden marriage to his uncle, Hamlet remarks:

> O, God! A beast that wants discourse of reason,
> Would have mourned longer[17]

Even Claudius reflects on what it is to be human when talking about Ophelia's madness:

> . . . poor Ophelia
> Divided from herself and her fair judgement,
> Without the which we are mere pictures, or mere beasts.[18]

The Spanish Tragedy is also full of imagery which compares human behaviour to that of animals. Lorenzo talks about the wooing of Belimperia, as if she were an animal to be tamed:

> In time the savage bull sustaines the yolk,
> In time all haggard hawks will stoop to lure,[19]

Hieronimo's final words in the play make it clear that his thirst for revenge has transformed him into something savage:

> But never shalt thou force me to reveal
> The thing that I have vowed inviolate,
> And therefore, in despite of all thy threats,
> Pleased with their deaths, and eased with their revenge,
> First take my tongue and afterwards my heart![20]

He then bites out his tongue, stabs the Duke and himself. Revenge has made Hieronimo become something other than human. He has been transformed into something wild and demonic; without any recognisable value system except revenge.

As Tillyard points out:

> The Elizabethans were interested in the nature of man with a fierceness rarely paralleled in other ages; and that fierceness delighted in exposing all the contrarieties in man's composition. In particular by picturing man's position between beast and angel with all possible emphasis they give a new intensity to the old conflict.[21]

Central to this conflict is the conviction that free will is what distinguishes human from animal, and conscience, reflection and self-awareness are central to this tension between human consciousness and animal impulsiveness. For the Elizabethans the moment of choice in the narrative takes on a cosmic significance. It is the moment when the hero is damning themselves. Not only is the protagonist choosing to behave in a way that is not human, he is also reliving the terrible choice made by Adam and Eve:

> For Understanding ruled not, and the Will
> Heard not her lore; both in subjection now
> To sensual Appetite, who from beneath
> Usurping over sovereign Reason claimed
> Superior sway.[22]

We can now see the importance of anagnorisis within the context of the tragedy; not only is accepting responsibility a part of the universal human experience, and something inherited from classical Greek Tragedy, but also it is an additional trait that distinguishes the human from the animal. Anagnorisis fits in with the Elizabethan religious sensibility. The stages of the Catholic sacrament of reconciliation involve confession, penance and then reconciliation which awards the soul a state of grace. The anagnorisis gives the character a chance to repent, and to acknowledge that he or she was responsible for making the wrong choice at a specific moment in time. The characters are given a moment of reflection in which they repent their actions and concede that they have behaved wrongly; like animals, they have chosen expediency over morality. Acknowledging their part in the action is part of the first stage to redemption.

Checklist

Here is a checklist if you are writing a narrative that has been inspired by an Elizabethan Revenge Tragedy:

- The Aristotelian description of the tragic hero:
  - The hero begins prosperous and well but ends up dead.
  - The hero's downfall is brought about by an error in judgement.
  - The hero will realize this and take responsibility.
- A murder will have been committed before the story begins (or right at the beginning of the story) and the protagonist will seek revenge.
- There will be violent action during the course of the narrative. (There may also be reported violence or death.)

- There will be the inclusion of supernatural elements and madness.

- Use will be made of meta-textuality (a play within a play or a film within a film).

- A new sense of order will be established at the end of the play that in some way justifies the violence.

- The central tension in the story will be that of human versus animal, or of morality versus expediency.

- Use will be made of forensic rhetoric – a character genuinely does not know what he will decide, and the act of talking about it helps him to make the decision.

5

MASHING IT UP: *DESPERATE HOUSEWIVES*, JACOBEAN TRAGEDY AND *BUFFY*

The excessive nature of Jacobean Tragedy is what makes it fun. It is always violent, graphic and bloody, and always in some dark way deeply entertaining. The excess exceeds our expectation and often our limits of what is bearable. These stories often have more blood and gore than we can think we can tolerate, and it is this pushing the boundaries which makes Jacobean Tragedy what it is. The evolution from Elizabethan Revenge Tragedy to Jacobean Tragedy is similar to that from Greek Tragedy to Roman Tragedy. Jacobean Tragedy evolves from Elizabethan Tragedy in several ways: madness and the supernatural are still present; violence becomes an even more prominent feature but, like Roman Tragedy, there is no need to provide a definite resolve in the order → chaos → reorder model; the inherent morality of the story is less clear; a confusion arises about what is comical and what is grotesquely violent; and the subplot has evolved into an almost separate parallel plot. In short the mechanics of the plot have become more elaborate, the morality less obvious and the violence pushed to a more extreme limit. It is the drama of excess. While early Elizabethan Tragedy is also excessive to some degree, Jacobean Tragedy is distinct in its use of parallel plots, and, as we shall see, in the way it portrays female sexuality.

The settings of Jacobean Tragedies are removed from the reality of the English audience which once enjoyed them. This is an important feature. In a Protestant England of the seventeenth century, the plays are always set in the Catholic environment of Italy or Spain. This exotic location is useful both politically and creatively. With the ongoing tensions still volatile between Catholics and Protestants, the plays may be seen to contain an element of propaganda which gives them a licence to show extreme behaviour. The depraved acts and savage behaviour which the plays portray are not happening among the *English* aristocracy, but among the ruling classes of continental Europe. This is indicative of how Catholics are inclined to behave according to a seventeenth-century Protestant perspective, and that is useful in appeasing those who have the power to keep the theatres and their box-offices open. Freed from any political restraints, the stories can be given a degree of creative freedom which would not have been possible if the setting were the English aristocracy of the time. The behaviour at the Italian court is less likely to be challenged, as so few of the audience will have first-hand experience of it, and, apart from the prejudicial attitudes, they are sufficiently removed from the audience's sensibilities. The writers therefore have licence to create a world which suits their story.

This is exactly what we encounter in many contemporary films and television programmes. For example, Quentin Tarantino always constructs a world which is clearly fictitious, even though it might at first appear familiar. In fact, the familiarity we experience when watching a Tarantino film is because of other fictitious worlds which the film references rather than an actual reality which they faithfully depict. For example, the world of *Django Unchained*[1] is not an authentic portrayal of nineteenth-century plantations in the southern states of the United States. It is an imaginative representation creating a fictional new world using tropes from westerns, blaxploitation films and horror. This is not to undermine the value of the discussion about slavery and racism that Tarantino is initiating, and like all his films, it contains a deeply moral sensibility. However, it is a heightened and fictionalized world that he creates, free from the pressures of being historically accurate. The examples of anachronisms in the film are numerous: dynamite had not been invented in 1858; there is a plastic clasp visible on a hat; neither the word 'genes' nor 'teddies' would have meant anything; cocktails are served that were not invented until the twentieth century. Like the seventeenth-century impression of Catholic aristocracy in Spain and Italy, it is the impression created that is important.

The starting point for Jacobean Tragedy is usually the same: the sexuality of a young woman. The Duchess in *The Duchess of Malfi*,[2] Beatrice Joanna in *The Changeling*,[3] Evadne in *The Maid's Tragedy*[4] and Annabella in *'Tis Pity She's a Whore*[5] are all examples of how a young woman's appetite for sexual experience is the springboard for the chaos of the story. Arguably, writing in the Jacobean period begins the categorisation of women into one of three types for the first time. Each female character is defined by her attitude to sexuality. The women are reduced to 'virgin', 'mother' and 'whore'. For a Jacobean audience, this serves their prejudice about Catholicism and their misunderstanding of the Catholic treatment of women. Catholicism is a religion which involves honouring Christ's mother, statues of the Virgin Mary, images portraying the naked body, vibrant colours and sensuous smells. To a Puritan mind, these elements of worship are signs of decadence and immodesty. Therefore it follows, according to this mindset, that the women who grow up in this culture are equally dubious in terms of their morality. Attacking the virtue of the women is also an effective way to discredit the entire culture which accompanies the religion. To a Jacobean audience, it is an opportunity to have their prejudice reinforced, but still explore salacious or titillating topics, a moral doublespeak, as they get to explore the forbidden stories while at the same time not being implicated in any sinning. Some might suggest that this attitude to women in our stories has not changed in the past four hundred years, and that women are still portrayed according to their sexuality, while men are not.

Let us take the television drama *Desperate Housewives*[6] as an example. This highly successful television comedy drama seems to be structured in a way that might make it belong to the Jacobean Tragedy lineage. Each murder is somehow the result – either directly or indirectly – of the impulses of a woman. Each of the main characters is clearly defined by a primitive view of female sexuality. The characters of Bree Van de Kamp, Lynette Scavo, Gabrielle Solis and Edie Britt are all distinct by their different views of sexuality. However, in accordance with our contemporary tastes, the stereotypes have evolved somewhat. While the mother figure remains and we remain fixated on the promiscuous female character, the virgin may be replaced by someone who appears prudish or frigid – like Bree Van de Kamp. In addition, the twentieth century produces an additional female stereotype: the victim. There is something seductive or alluring about this type of character, as if her suffering is attractive, and like the *femme fatal* – to whom she is related – there is every chance that the man she is attracted to will also suffer and be brought down. In *Desperate Housewives*, Susan Mayer fulfils this stereotype. It is important to state once again at this point that it is only the women who are defined in this way. The men in the stories may have more complex attributes independent of their sexuality, or even change and develop.

This way of stereotyping women has become so embraced by our culture that it is seen in stories that are not related to Jacobean Tragedy or its subsequent evolution. The highly successful comedy drama, *Sex and the City*,[7] also clearly categorizes the four women in the story according to these types. According to the morality of contemporary drama, the woman with the sexual appetite is the one who must suffer most. This was also the case in the narrative of Jacobean Tragedy four hundred years ago. The television comedy, *Girls*,[8] is notable by the way that women are not depicted in this way.

Exercise

Consider a plot in which the sexual appetites of a young woman unleash a sequence of events involving multiple murders. Is there a point where the young woman nearly gets away with it? How does the story end and what are the moral implications of this ending?

It might be suggested that there is a link between Jacobean Tragedy and the contemporary horror film. Unimaginable degrees of violence, the creation of a monster and a comment on female sexuality are common to both. The moral message is clear in both – promiscuity in a woman will lead to her destruction. Let us look at this meta-textual moment from the film *Scream*:

Randy: There are certain rules that one must abide by in order to successfully survive a horror movie. For instance, number one: you can never have sex.
(*The crowd boos*.)
Randy: Big no! Big no! Big no! Sex equals death, okay? Number two: you can never drink or do drugs.
(*The crowd cheers and raises their bottles*.)
Randy: The sin factor! It's a sin. It's an extension of number one.

It would seem, then, that both Jacobean Tragedy and the contemporary horror film are the result of a Puritan sensibility. They portray the world through a Puritan filter, and illustrate dramatically a point that the writer and activist Emma Goldman made in 1917:

Puritanism, in whatever expression, is a poisonous germ. On the surface everything may look strong and vigorous; yet the poison works its way persistently, until the entire fabric is doomed.[9]

Whether this is true for a Puritan culture is contentious, but it is certainly an accurate description of the stories in a Jacobean Tragedy – a Catholic setting seen from a puritanical perspective. Beneath a respectable and resilient public exterior lurks a private evil which persists until the culture supporting it is destroyed.

The plots of Jacobean Tragedy can sometimes be quite hard to recall. There is a reason for this. Before we examine exactly why this is, let us look in detail at the plot of *The Maid's Tragedy* by Beaumont and Fletcher.[10]

Melantius, a distinguished soldier, returns home to Rhodes to discover that his sister Evadne had been given to the young courtier Amintor by the king. This has left Aspatia, previously betrothed to Amintor, dejected and despairing. Melantius and Aspatia's father Calianax are seen by the king to be arguing before the wedding masque over Melantius' placement of a woman guest too close to the king. The king calls for peace. The wedding masque ensues.

As Evadne is being prepared for her wedding night, Aspatia pledges twice to kill herself: once in the presence of the bride and once to the bridegroom, her former betrothed, Amintor. He feels a pang of love for her. Evadne then reveals that she feels sick and is unable to sleep with her new husband. She eventually confesses that she has taken an oath never to sleep with Amintor, but remain true to another man: the king. The wedding is a ruse organized by the king so that Evadne may be mother to his children and retain her honour. She is currently pregnant with his child. As it is the king who has organized it, Amintor agrees to go along with this ruse for the time being. Aspatia remains in mourning, and Calianax, her father, pledges vengeance on both Amintor and Melantius.

Greeted by her brothers the following morning, Amintor tells of his fictitious night with Evadne. Evadne is offended by these necessary lies and accuses him of overdoing it. Her brothers suspect that something is wrong with Amintor, as he appears so sad. The king enters and suspects that all is not well with Amintor. Evadne reveals her ambition to be the mistress to the king, and explains how much she hates Amintor for coming between her and the king. Amintor accuses the king of tyranny, but also pledges his obedience, as a subject should. Meanwhile Calianax draws and challenges Melantius while Melantius is trying to make an ally of him. He backs down when he realizes that youth is no longer on his side. Melantius then asks Amintor why he is acting so manically. Melantius explains that their friendship is at stake if Amintor does not reveal the cause of his behaviour. Amintor weeps uncontrollably at the thought of losing his friend over this matter. He explains the matter. Melantius draws his sword and challenges him for calling his sister a 'whore'. Reluctantly Amintor also draws, which makes Melantius realize that he is telling the truth. Melantius pledges vengeance on his behalf. Amintor perceives this as wrong, and challenges him to fight, to prevent him fighting the king and revealing Amintor's shame to the world. Melantius draws, but then backs down for the love of his friend, deceiving Amintor that he will take no action. Both brothers, Melantius and Diphilus, swear vengeance on the king. Melantius asks Calianax for help also, knowing that the he will go straight to the king and tell of the revolt.

Melantius forces Evadne to confess to him, in a violent scene, and as her penance, she is to kill the king. Evadne then prostrates herself before Amintor, asking for his forgiveness. There is reconciliation between them. Amintor kisses her farewell vowing there will be no further contact between them. Calianax tells the king of the plot. All are called before the king for a wedding banquet. With friendly banter the king broaches the topic of killing a king. Melantius is presumed innocent as he fails to show guilt, and Calianax is perceived to be in the wrong. Calianax is warned by the king not to make this mistake again. Amintor tells Melantius that he wants revenge immediately – as the king has just called Evadne to him. Melantius tells him to be wary and wait for the right opportunity, as it is not possible to kill a king and get away with it.

Evadne goes to the king while he is sleeping and ties his arms to the bed. She stabs him three times. His body is discovered. Melantius has the fort. The king's brother, Lysippus, reluctantly declares himself king. Melantius asks Calianax, now his prisoner, to talk to the people from the fort as his power of rhetoric is so effective. Lysippus gives Melantius the chance to confess and end this revolt if he gives up the fort. Dressed as a man Aspatia goes to see Amintor. She tells him that she is her brother who has come to revenge the wrongs done to her sister, hoping that he will kill her in a fight. She hits him. He does not retaliate. She kicks him. They fight. She allows herself to be wounded and falls to the ground. Evadne enters covered in blood and announces that she has murdered the king. She wishes for Amintor to take her to his bed. He rejects her. She kills herself. Amintor expresses his desire to return to Aspatia. She hears this as she lies dying, and reveals herself to him. Filled with hope, Aspatia wishes to live, but dies of the wound Amintor gave her. Amintor stabs himself. The rest of the court discovers the dead. Melantius goes to kill himself, but is restrained. Melantius swears he will starve himself to death.

The plot is complex, and involved. It consists of many twists and turns. Reveals and peripety are commonplace throughout the story: a celebrated soldier returns to a disagreement rather than a celebration; a wedding night turns into a traumatic event as hope turns to disappointment; a loyal subject turns into a murderous rebel; a night of love-making turns into a torture and murder scene. There are many examples of accusation followed by recanting, or characters threatening to fight and then withdrawing. Throughout the play, suspicion frequently turns into belief. The most extreme of these turnarounds happens at the very end of the play: Aspatia disguising herself as her brother, and then revealing herself; Amintor revealing his love for Aspatia, but he has already fatally wounded her, and she has decided she now wants to live. Animosity turns into love as a will to die turns into a will to live. This use of peripety is audacious, and causality might be considered the sacrifice. The audience remains entertained and involved throughout, as each turnaround brings with it surprise or shock, but the careful organic nature of the story developing is no longer a matter for consideration.

We first encountered the notion of peripety in connection with Greek Tragedy – a form in which a character might experience one major peripety in the space of the whole narrative, rather than one per scene. The price is causality. In fact, causality is often lost to such a degree that when we come to the end of some Jacobean Tragedies, we feel a sense of bewilderment at the events. It seems that in these cases, enjoyment eclipses our sense of belief, and we cease to question what has happened because we have enjoyed watching it unravel. However, on reflection, we realize that the writer has in some way generated the excitement of the fast-moving plot, rather than it being a connection between cause and effect. This is often the case with current television. The need for peripety exceeds the need for integrity in telling the story. This is especially the case if a commercial break is interrupting the narrative at frequent intervals. I often find that I have enjoyed a whole season of *Breaking Bad*, *Desperate Housewives*, *The Sopranos*, or even *The Vampire Diaries*, but I am unable to recall the details of the complete season's story arc. A good character has turned bad, or a bad character has redeemed themselves, and it is no longer entirely clear how it happened. It would appear that according to the tastes of contemporary popular storytelling, peripety is more important than causality. Some writers are known for their ability to take us by surprise with their use of the turnaround, for example, Russel T. Davies, Stephen Moffat, Joss Whedon, Kevin Williamson and J. J. Abrams. Perhaps J. J. Abrams's *Lost*[11] is the most extreme example of what happens when periperty exceeds causality: a world is created which is somewhat elusive and in which anything can happen.

Exercise

Write a scene which involves a turnaround as extreme as one that has featured in a Jacobean Tragedy. Concentrate on the causality of this transformation, and try to avoid anything too sudden which compromises the integrity of the scene. If you wish, make the polemic shift something subtle. It needn't be love turning to hate, or life turning to death; it might also be loyalty turning into betrayal or innocence turning into corruption.

Peripety has been discussed as being an important feature of the narrative when looking at other forms of tragedy. However, as we might imagine from such an excessive form as Jacobean Tragedy, its use is even more frequent than in Roman Tragedy and it seems to be one of the impulses driving the narrative. Almost every scene involves a peripety of some sort. This leads us to the use of comedy in Jacobean Tragedy. The violence and tragedy coexist with various comic tones: buffoonery, the grotesque, bawdy, verbal wit, dramatic irony. Often this is a matter of taste. Some audience members find the death of Aspatia at the hands of Amintor at the end of *The Maid's Tragedy* distressing and sad; others find it funny. The use of reveal and turnaround is so extreme, and the plotting so blatant that something comical emerges from the apparent incongruity of form and content – what is happening seems at odds with how it is happening. Of course it is possible that some audience members find it both funny and tragic. This is the feeling that a Tarantino film evokes, for example. We are never quite sure when the gun will go off. In *Pulp Fiction*,[12] Vincent shoots Marvin accidentally in the car while they are discussing matters of faith. In *Django Unchained*, Dr Schultz shoots Calvin Candie at a completely unexpected moment, unleashing a torrent of violence in the excessively bloody shoot-out that follows. The torture scene in *The Maid's Tragedy* seems to anticipate the tone of a Tarantino film. Evadne goes to the king's bedchamber, and ties him up while he is sleeping. He wakes up and assumes that this is part of an erotic game. However, he ends up being stabbed multiple times and dies pleading with her for mercy.

> **King:** Thou dost not mean this; tis impossible;
>   Thou art too sweet and gentle.
> **Evadne:** No, I am not,
>   I am as foul as thou art, and can number
>   As many such hells here. I was once fair,
>   Once I was lovely, not a blowing rose
>   More chastely sweet, till thou, thou foul canker –
>   Stir not! – didst poison me.[13]

The situation is comic because of the incongruity, and this incongruity is brought about by the abundance of peripety converging in this one scene: a loyal subject becomes a rebel; a lover becomes a murderer; an arrogant man is debased to the point where he has to plead for pity; a murder is viewed as a method of redemption. In addition, there is the incongruity of tone – an act of murder is being depicted with a tone that is almost light-hearted. However, there is also a comic element caused by it being so excessively grotesque: the tyrannical and bullying king is made to plead pitifully for his life while he is stabbed multiple times.

Exercise

Write a scene that might be seen as comically violent. Use one of the following techniques to establish the comedy:

- Incongruity of tone and content – the tone is light-hearted, but the content is heavy.
- Repeated use of peripety – build in many turnarounds into your scene that the comedy comes from a feeling of disbelief.
- Push the boundary of violence and horror to a degree that it becomes grotesquely funny. Please note: there are certain things that can never be funny according to cultural taste. It is always safer to see a powerful figure subjected to this treatment than someone who is weak, or is already considered a victim.

Buffy the Vampire Slayer[14] mixed genres in a way reminiscent of Jacobean Tragedy. A dramatic scene concerning unrequited love would be followed by a horror scene involving vampires. This in turn would be followed by a scene of heightened comedy or buffoonery involving Xander and Anya. The episode, *Once*

More with Feeling,[15] makes the 'mash-up' of genres even more rich; a demon arrives in Sunnydale who makes the residents spontaneously burst into song. This excessive layering of narrative tone is representative of the spirit of Jacobean Tragedy – it does not restrict itself to one mode if it can amalgamate several.

Another element common to both Jacobean Tragedy and the modern horror film is the creation of a monster. The brothers in *The Duchess of Malfi*, De Flores in *The Changeling*, Giovanni in *'Tis Pity She's a Whore* are all monsters that are equal to those such as Freddie from the *Friday The 13th* franchise or Hannibal Lector from *The Silence of the Lambs*[16] and other episodes from this series. These monsters share a psychopathic characteristic: they are void of any empathy, and are not able to assess the morality of the situation at hand in quite the way that we would expect if they were rational human beings. They do not share a common appreciation of what is right and what is wrong. In Shakespeare's tragedies we see a tension between animal behaviour and human behaviour; or between expediency and morality. Jacobean Tragedy takes the notion of a monster to an extreme, and this is one of the sources of its enjoyment. We get to see behaviour pushed to a boundary which surpasses our expectation. The principles that make us human are absent, as these characters reject common morality, but they surpass even animals in their behaviour. They will lie instinctively, murder indiscriminately or sleep with anyone they sexually desire – *anyone*, even their own sister (or a dead woman in the case of *The Second Maiden's Tragedy*[17]). Unable to empathize, refusing to adapt, oblivious to the boundaries and rules that keep society safe, these characters have sociopathic traits that are shocking. Perhaps, the very essence of a Jacobean Tragedy concerns identifying the face of the monster, and the shocking revelation is that he or she looks just like us. This is reminiscent of the *Alien* films. The aliens are terrifying, but more terrifying are the corporate-style military who wish to cultivate the aliens as weapons of mass destruction – the human face of unwavering evil is the most terrifying monster of all.

Exercise

Write a scene in which the audience realize that they are indeed watching a monster. Choose the moments to reveal the details and remember to keep it credible.

These tragedies are so excessive that often the plot cannot be contained in a single thread, and two concurrent threads are involved. These parallel plots rarely (if ever) converge. In *The Maids Tragedy*, there is the plot involving Evadne, Aspatia and Amintor, and also the plot concerning the argument between Melantius and Calianax.

The moral implications of the way the story ends are complex. Like Roman Tragedy, there is no reordering beyond the fact that evil has extinguished itself. Sometimes we have the feeling that evil has triumphed. Even though the evil characters have died, the innocent have perished also. We are left with a sense of futility and waste. There is no new hope. As in Roman Tragedy, this desperate sense of an ending can be strangely satisfying.

Checklist

Here is a checklist if your model for writing your play or film is Jacobean Tragedy:

- This is an excessive form in many ways: violence, multiple plot strands, madness are all common features.

- The story begins with the sexuality of a young woman which then unleashes chaos.

- During the story, a monster is created which exceeds the audience's expectations.

- Comedy and violence mix together.

- Aristotle's description for the tragic hero is still relevant. It is essential that the young woman has a moment of anagnorisis (recognition that she is to blame).

- The use of peripety is frequent. There will be at least one turnaround in every scene.

- No resolve is needed except the destruction of all who have been affected by the violence.

- You may, if you wish, include a religious setting, or place the story in a religious context.

6

THE PLATE OF SARDINES: NEW GREEK COMEDY, MENANDER AND *FRASIER*

Comedy of Action is distinct from character-based comedy. In Comedy of Action the audience's response arises from the situation that the characters find themselves in, and it is the arising problem that requires a solution. While the characters themselves may be intriguing or amusing, it is their action in the situation which causes the audience to laugh. This distinction may be a little blurred at times, but generally most comedy can be sorted into one of two distinct types: Comedy of Action or Comedy of Character. Here are some examples:

Character Comedy	Action Comedy
Aristophanes – Old Comedy	Menander – New Comedy
Wycherly – *The Country Wife*	Shakespeare – *The Comedy of Errors*
The Plays of Oscar Wilde	The Plays of Feydeau
Ayckbourn – *Absurd Person Singular*	Frayn – *Noises Off*
Ab Fab	*Frasier*
The Office	*Curb your Enthusiasm*
Keeping up Appearances	*Seinfeld*

Naturally, there is an overlap. Sometimes there is action in character comedy, and sometimes the characters in action comedy seem to be funny in their own right. As we examine the impulses of comedy over the next four chapters, this somewhat theoretical distinction will become clearer. The term 'farce' has been avoided in this chapter. While the terms 'farce' and 'comedy of action' are synonymous, the word 'farce' can often bring with it preconceived notions of what style or content is involved.

Menander was a Greek dramatist living between 342 and 291 BC. Only one of his plays survives in its entirety, *Dyskolos* or *Old Cantankerous*.[1] Only fragments of the other plays exist. Despite these plays being over 2,000 years old, many seem remarkably contemporary – perhaps even familiar. The reason for this is perhaps that the rules of certain types of comedy have not changed. Whether it is a play by Menander or an episode of *Frasier*,[2] the fundamental structure is the same.

There is perhaps a parallel to be drawn between the enjoyment that we experience from watching a tragedy and the enjoyment that we experience from watching a Comedy of Action. In tragedy we find it somehow pleasurable to empathize with someone else's experiences of separation and grief while watching the downfall from well-being to destruction, and in Comedy of Action we enjoy witnessing someone else's experiences of panic while watching their potential downfall. This is the fundamental pleasure of watching these comedies: our experience of someone else's panic is visceral and the way we breathe changes as we anticipate the impending disaster. In the chapters on tragedy, we examined the way a story progresses by the main character engaging with a process of:

$$choice \rightarrow consequence \rightarrow change$$

What makes Comedy of Action so pleasurable and also sometimes exasperating is that the choices are frequently made in an increasing hurry. The characters are given no time to reflect; they must act swiftly as the plot progresses and the sense of panic escalates.

In Menander's *The Girl from Samos*,[3] Demeas returns home from a business trip of many months to discover that his common-law wife, Chrysis, has given birth to a baby. The baby is not in fact theirs, but Chrysis is claiming that it is until Demeas's son Moschion can get married to his girlfriend in order to save them the embarrassment of having an illegitimate child at the wedding and putting Demeas's agreement to the marriage in jeopardy. All the servants are aware of the truth, and Demeas overhears a kitchenmaid telling someone that the Moschion is the father of the child. He immediately assumes that his son has had an affair with his wife. Before the muddle is cleared up, Chrysis is made homeless, Moschion is disinherited and Demeas nearly fights the neighbour in a duel. The play ends with Moschion and his girlfriend getting married, Chrysis being forgiven and Demeas admitting his folly for being so suspicious.

An initial choice made by Moschion and Chrysis has a consequence which then leads to Demeas making a series of assumptions and choices which nearly results in crisis. This, in short, is the structure of Comedy of Action.

In the television comedy, *Frasier*, a situation often has Frasier, Niles or Martin work themselves up into such a state that panic is induced and there is an extravagant explosion of frustration and rage. In the episode *The Two Mrs Cranes*,[4] Daphne pretends that Niles is her husband in order to avoid an awkward situation with an ex-boyfriend. Roz is caught up in the deceit, pretending to be Frasier's wife, 'Lilith'. Martin exploits the situation by pretending to be an astronaut. When the ex-boyfriend reveals that he is now a successful businessman, Daphne and Roz compete for his attention despite his now believing that they are both married. They do this by making up unattractive details about each other, and announcing these indiscretions over the dinner table. The story culminates in the ex-boyfriend lecturing them about what terrible people they are and storming out of the apartment.

Through this process of hurried decision making, both Demeas and the characters in *Frasier* are inevitably led to a climactic crisis in which something serious and terrible nearly occurs. There is then a denouement or 'unknotting' in which the whole muddle is resolved and a sense of calm is restored. Comedy of Action follows the same central pattern that we have already examined when looking at tragedy:

$$order \rightarrow chaos \rightarrow reorder$$

The elements of Comedy of Action have remained the same throughout the centuries. This type of comedy always begins with a muddle – something is concealed or something is misunderstood. This muddle develops into chaos, and a crisis is narrowly avoided by a last-minute solution which then leads to the reordering.

In *The Girl from Samos*, Moschion conceals the fact that the baby is really his, and this leads Demeas to misunderstand the situation, and believe that his son is having an affair with his wife. In *Frasier*, Daphne conceals the fact that she is still a single woman, and misses out on the opportunity to reconnect with an old boyfriend. Roz, Niles and Frasier are all insulted and made to look like fools in the process. The situation that arises from this concealment or misunderstanding is often called 'the *game*'. It is Demeas's thinking that his son is the father of a newly born baby, or in the episode of *Frasier*, it is Daphne trying to chat up an ex-boyfriend even though she has to compete with Roz, and he thinks that she is married to Niles. If an effective and amusing *game* is established it can often be repeated over and over again, and the comedy remains fresh and interesting. This leads us to one of the tricks of Comedy of Action: the *game* must be established as quickly and as economically as possible. Look at the way it is handled in Menander's play: Moschion comes on stage and delivers a monologue explaining what has happened. This exposition, delivered economically and without any fuss, contains all the audience needs to know to appreciate and enjoy the *game*.

The next three exercises all involve constructing a Comedy of Action. It is important that you avoid writing or devising a character-based comedy. For the exercises, please use only regular, apparently normal characters, rather than characters with heightened comedic traits. You may even write a character based on yourself or versions of yourself. This will ensure that the comedy arises from the context, and not from the characters being funny.

Exercise

Consider a situation which involves concealment and misunderstanding which might then lead to the sort of muddle that you find in Comedy of Action. How are you going to communicate this information to the audience, so that they understand the rules and can enjoy the game as quickly as possible? Come up with two different possibilities of handling this exposition. If possible try to move the action forward while simultaneously explaining the rules of the game. In addition to these versions, write a version that involves a monologue being given in direct address to the audience.

Unlike in this exercise, you may find, when you write a play or a screenplay, that you are tempted to somehow deviate from the essential information because you fear that the exposition will be too dry or monotonous. This is understandable, and can be resolved by positioning the exposition within the narrative structure. If the exposition is positioned as the second scene or element in your narrative, then for the first element, you can employ a *narrative hook*. Many plays, films and television sitcoms use this technique. A narrative hook is a stand-alone piece of action which has no immediate relevance to the rest of the narrative. Its purpose is solely to hook the audience and engage them with the world of the story. The device is not only used in comedies. James Bond films and other action films employ extravagant and elaborate narrative hooks to involve the audience. Every episode of *Frasier, Friends, Parks and Recreation* or the US version of *The Office* begins with a narrative hook, the action of which does not necessarily have anything to do with the scene which follows.

Exercise

Write an opening for a comedy. The purpose of this opening is to grab the audience's attention and involve them in the world of the story. Use the same characters and context as you used for the previous exercise. What situation would get an audience immediately hooked? Can you involve heightened emotions (e.g. a sudden cry of panic, or an outburst of rage or fear)? Is there a way of seamlessly linking this scene to your scene of exposition?

In Comedy of Action, a good *game* can be played many times without the audience tiring of it. Each time they enjoy understanding what is happening even though the characters remain unaware of the full picture. Anticipating the results of any concealment or misunderstanding is one of the pleasures of this type of comedy. Here is a useful model for how the narrative develops:

1 Following the exposition, the *game* is played the first time in order to establish the rules and show the consequences of what has been revealed in the set-up.

2 The *game* is then played a second time and the stakes are increased slightly. From an audience perspective, this is enjoyable as the rules of the *game* are now clear.

3 The *game* is then played a third time, and this time the narrative develops to a point of panic or crisis. By this time, the audience may have forgotten the dramatic irony (that they understand more than the characters) and will be experiencing the same sense of panic that the characters are experiencing. The stakes here must be high: the potential disaster which is the consequence of the *game* might be utter humiliation, or violence, or a break-up, or abandonment.

4 At the point of crisis, a denouement occurs. This is usually the result of a turnaround which might be as simple as the main character realising that there has been a misunderstanding. It could also be the revelation of a completely new piece of information. This brings with it a sense of relief; the audience breathes differently as the world of the narrative is once again ordered and no longer in chaos.

The *game* may change slightly each time it is played. Even though it is based on the same misunderstanding or concealment, the rules may change slightly because of something that happened the previous time the *game* was played.

Exercise

Write a sequence of scenes in which the *game* is played three times according to the suggested structure: once to establish it, once for enjoyment and once to bring the situation to a crisis. Then, at the point of crisis, introduce a denouement which restores order and relief.

The preceding three exercises will produce a prototype Comedy of Action. This might be one long scene, operating in real time, or it might consist of five different scenes. It will involve each of these five stages:

1 Narrative hook

2 Exposition: the rules of the game are explained

3 Game played for the first time: to establish it

4 Game played for the second time: for enjoyment

5 Game played for the third time: to induce crisis, followed by the resolve and reordering at the last minute

Here are some tips to help enhance the narrative and the comedy:

1 Relentless panic or confusion becomes monotonous after a while – the heightened parts of the scene must be punctuated with quieter moments.

2 In this type of writing reactions are as important as actions.

3 The audience must have time to watch the characters making decisions. Even though many decisions are made in a hurry in this type of comedy, it is important that we have a sense that the decision could go either way.

Let us examine some typical elements of Comedy of Action in more depth. These are the essential impulses and building blocks which drive Comedy of Action.

Dramatic Irony

The audience understands, but the characters do not. This is one of the essential mechanisms of this type of comedy. Although dramatic irony is employed in other genres, the audience experiences a suspenseful expectation of something happening – either funny or disastrous – but the characters remain largely unaware. Murray H. Abrams points out:

> the character acts in a way that is grossly inappropriate to the actual circumstances, or expects the opposite of what we know.[5]

When characters behave in this way, effective comedy occurs. The audience laughs from a position of slight superiority. However, as the *game* is played again and again, and the stakes increase, the impact of the dramatic irony on the audience decreases and the audience's involvement in the characters' panic and impending crisis becomes prevalent.

The Concealment

Concealment is one of the devices which adds to the pleasure of dramatic irony. Something is concealed, of which the audience are aware, but the characters are not. This could be information (someone is convincingly pretending to be of the opposite gender, someone is experiencing a secret unrequited love, someone has an identical twin), or it might be based around an object (a letter, a locket, a plate of sardines). This is why props are often so important and plentiful in Comedy of Action. The comedy is most effective when the reason for the concealment is convincing, and the price that will be paid, if the concealment is revealed, must be significant.

Exercise

Consider and write a plot outline for an action comedy using the notion of concealment. Use the structure that we have already discussed: think of a game, set it up with an exposition scene, play the game three times to take the narrative to crisis and then resolve it all with a denouement.

Cross-purpose and Misunderstanding

While cross-purpose and misunderstanding may be the result of something concealed, this mechanism of comedy is not dependent on it. It simply requires someone to 'get the wrong end of the stick', and then become convinced that they are right and so inflexible about changing their opinion. In The *Girl from Samos*, Demeas overhears the cook, and assumes that his son is having an affair with his wife. All the evidence he gathers during the course of the play seems to support this misunderstanding. There is an episode of *Frasier* which illustrates this device clearly. In the episode, *The Ski Lodge*,[6] Frasier and Niles take Martin, Daphne and Daphne's friend Annie away to a ski lodge. The complications are increased by a ski instructor also staying there. Owing to various misunderstandings, each character wrongly believes that another character wants to sleep with them. Guy, the ski instructor, and Annie are both attracted to Niles and think that he is interested in them, Niles thinks that Daphne is interested in him and Frasier thinks that Annie is interested in him. Meanwhile, Guy believes Annie and Daphne to be a same-sex couple. The denouement follows a particularly manic sequence and involves Frasier realising that, in fact, no one found him attractive. No props are involved nor are there complicated details; the *game* is a simple case of multiple misunderstandings culminating in Frasier's inevitable disappointment. One of the key elements to the way the character interacts with the world is that they display inflexibility, and this becomes a source of the comedy. The game would be shorter and the comedy would make less of an impact if either Frasier or Basil Fawlty were capable of changing their point of view. They are inflexible in the way they think and the surprises of the ever changing situation demands flexibility of thought. This simple character trait maximizes the comic potential for the misunderstanding.

Genuine Surprise: The Reveal or Turnaround

This narrative technique is a way of creating a new complication in the course of the comedy, or a way of bringing about the denouement at the end. A piece of previously unknown information is revealed to both audience and characters. This new information changes everything. The delight of this device is that everyone makes the discovery at the same time; both audience and characters have to deal with change; there is the shock of new circumstances or an assumption has to be dismissed. The turnaround elicits a physical response in the audience, either of panic or of relief. The German philosopher Immanuel Kant explains that our laughter arises from 'the sudden transformation of a strained expectation into nothing'. At the end of Shakespeare's *The Comedy of Errors*, the abbess is revealed to be Emilia, the wife of Egeon and the mother of the twins. This reveal provides a resolution – a crisis is avoided and a new order is established. In an episode of *Fawlty Towers*,[7] there is a reveal which is devastating for the viewer and protagonist alike. *Gourmet Night*[8] culminates with a reveal right at the very end of the episode which ensures the humiliation of Basil Fawlty.

As in the use of peripety, when we discussed tragedy, the turnaround must be used sparingly by the writer. There is a psychological contract between the audience and the storyteller that they will be able to trust the world of the narrative, as this world mostly obeys rules that we can rely on. Causality and integrity are at stake. The American television comedy *Arrested Development*[9] is breathtaking in its invention. However, the turnarounds happen too rapidly, and so, while the viewer still finds it very funny, they perhaps begin to distrust the integrity of a world in which anything can happen. As Aristotle points out in *Poetics*, 'the unravelling of the plot, no less than the complication, must arise out of the plot itself, it must not be brought about by the Deus ex Machina'.

Misfortune

It is important in comedy that the potential for misfortune is somehow present. Without this there are no stakes, and so the audience remain less involved. The misfortune might involve divorce, a friendship ending, physical danger, violence, humiliation or disgrace. Within this form of comedy, there are some types of character that occur often:

1 Someone who is hungry and penniless
2 Someone who is proud, pompous and bombastic
3 Someone who is volatile and teetering on the brink of rage

We explore character types in the following chapter, but we can see already that these characters keep misfortune close: starvation, humiliation and violence are all real possibilities.

Time Limits

Our sense of panic increases when we watch someone making decisions in a hurry. This in turn increases the visceral response of, and therefore comic potential for, the audience.

Exercise

Write a scene in which something must be resolved by a certain time limit. Include three characters and ensure that the main element preventing the resolve is an external one. For example, someone has to get a letter sent off by a certain time, but the envelopes are missing. Introduce an additional obstacle which comes from one of the characters. For example, another character is about to use the last envelope for her mother's birthday card. This mixture of external and internal impulses makes for a satisfying situation.

This exercise requires the writer to only focus on the action of the scene. All extraneous detail is irrelevant. Economy is demanded if the scene is to succeed. This task requires focus on the constituent events and absence of any supplementary events. The sense of panic for the actors and the audience in this exercise, when it is performed well, is palpable and enjoyable. Audience and actors get more and more agitated as the time runs out and they share a sense of relief when the denouement occurs and the time limit is up.

Convergence of the Incompatible

When two things are forced together that normally would never go together, there is the potential for comedy. This might involve two types of people: country folk with city-dwellers, environmentalists with non-environmentalists, vegetarians with meat-eaters, an opera-lover with rock fans. Alternatively it might be a person (or people) converging with a situation with which they are otherwise incompatible: someone with a pollen allergy in a florists, someone on a strict diet in a cake shop, a drunk clown at a children's birthday party. The incompatibility need not be obvious to all the characters in the scene; often the comedy will arise from someone trying to conceal the truth and trying to accommodate and adapt. This is the stock currency of many American situation comedies: *Frasier*, *New Girl,*[10] *Curb Your Enthusiasm*[11] all thrive on the pathological incompatible converging in nearly every episode.

Some additional structural elements are worth investigation. The first is the *lazzi* which comes from the Italian word *lazzo*, and is an independent pre-rehearsed comic sequence. The lazzi is important in action comedy because it serves as a distraction or interlude in the narrative. It has nothing to do with the plot of the story, and, like a sketch, could be a stand-alone piece of comedy. This comedy might be physical:

- saving crockery from breaking
- enjoying trying on someone else's clothes
- trying to stop a chair from wobbling or a door from squeaking

or it might be verbal:

- the inability to say a particular word (the abominable snowman)
- a sequence of puns
- a monologue (see Dromio's speech in *The Comedy of Errors* about Nell, the Kitchen-maid)

The lazzi provides a change in rhythm from the *game* being played again and again. It is often placed after the *game* has been played for the first time, but in *Frasier*, it is often positioned directly after the exposition.

The structure that we have examined so far is a simple one in which the *game* is played three times to bring about a crisis. There is a variation in which the *game* changes each time. This follows the form:

$$\text{set-up} \rightarrow \text{development} \rightarrow \text{complication}$$

As in the previous model, the *game* is played the first time so that the audience can understand the fundamentals. This then develops into a different *game* but with the same characters and similar themes. A further development then happens which takes us into a new *game* and a crisis. In *A Servant to Two Masters*,[12] (or its contemporary update, *One Man, Two Guvners*[13]) Goldoni follows this model. However, he does so with two strands of narrative – Goldoni is writing two *games* at the same time.

Set-up 1: Truffaldino is serving two masters: Florindo and Beatrice. Neither knows about the other one; both think that they have his exclusive service.

Set-up 2: Beatrice is disguised as her brother, Federigo, in order to get the money owed to him. Her brother has been killed by her lover, Florindo. Both have arrived in Venice without knowing of the other's whereabouts.

Development 1: Truffaldino is unable to read, so rather than serving two masters, he is unable to serve either master. He gives money meant for Federigo (Beatrice) to the wrong master, Florindo. Beatrice discovers that the money is missing.

Development 2: Florindo is told that Federigo is still alive and has come to Venice. It is, of course, Beatrice disguised as Federigo.

Complication 1: Truffaldino mixes up the trunks, and tells each master that the other is dead. As both has proof, and Truffaldino's word – each decides to kill themselves.

Complication 2: Silvio believes that Clarice has promised Federigo (Beatrice) that she will marry him. He spurns her (after losing in a duel to Beatrice). She threatens to kill herself. When Silvio appears unmoved, she decides that she will marry Federigo (Beatrice) after all.

Denouement 1: Federigo reveals to Pantaloon that she is in fact a woman. Pantaloon can now sort out the mess with the young lovers.

Denouement 2: Beatrice and Florindo discover each other, as they are trying to hang themselves.

Denouement 3: Both realise that Truffaldino is serving each of them and that Pasquale (a fictional servant used as cover) does not exist.

Each time a game is played, it has at its root two elements of the original game: Truffaldino concealing the fact that he serves two people and Beatrice concealing her true identity. However, each time the game is played, an additional element is included to make each game different. The misfortune which could arise from this situation is grave: three characters threaten to commit suicide, and two of them even come close to attempting it. This seriousness makes the stakes high and provides a counterpoint to the comedy. This is a complicated and intricate narrative and in order to provide a variety of rhythm and distractions for the audience, Goldoni includes three *lazzi*:

Lazzi 1: The bread as glue

Lazzi 2: The money bill as an example of how to set the table

Lazzi 3: Serving two meals at once.

Like a magician performing a sleight-of-hand illusion, these distractions serve to have the audience 'take their eye off the ball'. The mechanics of the plot are less likely to become apparent when the plot is interrupted by these other highly enjoyable comic episodes.

Modern American television comedy is no less complex and ambitious than a play by Goldoni. *Friends*, *Seinfeld*, *Modern Family* and *Curb your Enthusiasm* all involve three different *games* being played simultaneously. In some of these cases, there is a regular cast of six so that the characters can be split up into three *games* involving two characters each. In the case of *Curb your Enthusiasm* and *Seinfeld*, the three *games* converge in the final scene to create a grand finale of confusion and crisis.

Exercise

Consider three games that can be played simultaneously. You do not need six characters for this – as we see in *Curb your Enthusiasm*, the same character can be involved in all three games. Allow yourself a maximum of twelve short scenes in which to complete the narrative which includes all three plot strands. If you are able, aim to complete it in nine scenes.

Comedy of Action is one of the most challenging genres to write or devise. It can be terrifying for the writers and performers, and highly stressful for the audience. Comedy is unique in that if it is not working, the performers are immediately aware of it, as they are failing to get laughs from the audience. It requires a remarkable discipline. The writer must commit to the *game* absolutely, and the *game* itself must be immediately understandable to the audience. However, when it works, the rewards for the audience, writer and performer are perhaps like no other to be had in any other mode or genre.

Checklist

Here is a checklist in case you wish to use the model of Comedy of Action for your own narrative.

- The exposition must be handled as swiftly as possible. This often happens at the expense of creativity.

- The success of this comedy depends on a simple but effective *game*, which can be played repeatedly.

- Use simple recognisable characters rather than heightened comic characters.

- The game might develop each time it is played into a slightly different game.

- Take the story to a point of crisis before providing a denouement to the muddle.

- This genre demands economy. Avoid any supplementary events.

- Turnarounds, reveals, time limits and the convergence of the incompatible are all techniques employed to build the narrative.

7
ARCHETYPE OR STEREOTYPE? PLAUTUS, COMEDY OF CONTRADICTIONS AND *THE SKETCH SHOW*

As we move from the comedy of the Greek playwright Menander to the Roman playwright Plautus, one innovation becomes clear. Plautus's plays take the plot structure from Menander, but add the characters of the Atellan farces. These were improvised comedies featuring lower-class characters, full of vulgarity, buffoonery and rude jokes. The plays were populated with stock characters including a fat man, a doddery old man, a Harlequin-type clown and a greedy clown.

While Greek New Comedy features stock characters to some degree, Roman New Comedy develops these even further: the Old Man (Senex); the Young Woman (Virgo); The Clever Slave (Servus Callidus); The Braggart Soldier (Miles Gloriosus). On first examination, if we look at the character types that Plautus employs in *The Pot of Gold*,[1] we can see how the characters seem to embody and develop these stock characters. The play involves Euclio (a miser) who has found a pot of gold in his house and his daughter Staphyla (a young woman) who is secretly in love with Lyconides. Following the exposition, which is told to the audience directly by Lars Familiaris, the guardian spirit of the house, we find Euclio kicking his old (but clever and trustworthy) servant out of his house so that he can check that the pot of gold is still there. We then meet Eunomia (an opinionated middle-aged woman) and her brother, Megadorus, Lyconides' uncle (an old man). Eunomia is encouraging her brother to marry, and Megadorus has his sights set on Staphyla, the unsuitably young daughter of Euclio. Throughout the action, Euclio is convinced that anyone he meets knows about the money, and he has to reassure them that he is still a poor man. Megadorus manages to convince Euclio, who sees it as a way of getting rid of his daughter without paying a dowry. The wedding is arranged for that day. Megadorus's servant, Strobilus (another clever servant), organizes the various staff. The pot of gold is moved around by Euclio in order to keep it hidden, and he refuses to spend any money at all on the wedding, even on his own outfit for the ceremony. Lyconides (the young lover thwarted in love) begs his mother to speak with his uncle and persuade him not to marry Staphyla. Meanwhile Lyconides' slave, Euclides (a witty but dishonourable servant), has overheard Euclio talking about the pot of gold and has successfully stolen it. Euclides and Lyconides then talk at cross-purposes: Euclides talks about his suffering owing to the stolen money, while Lyconides thinks that he has discovered that his daughter is pregnant and is talking about that. Inadvertently Lyconides leads Euclio to believe that he has stolen the money:

> **Lyconides:** It was some divine power that drove me to it, that tempted me to take what was not mine.[2]

They realize that they are talking at cross-purposes, and Lyconides confesses that he is responsible for Staphyla's pregnancy. The slave confesses to Lyconides that he has stolen the money, but refuses to give it back. Euclio stops the wedding preparations and dismisses the cooks. Lyconides returns with the slave and the pot of gold. Euclio agrees to the marriage and gives the pot of gold to Lyconides as a dowry for his daughter. In avoiding the responsibility of wealth, Euclio claims that he will be much happier as a pauper.

> **Megadorus:** There speaks a wise man. Contentment, peace of mind, and sound sleep at night are worth more than a dozen pots of gold.[3]

In terms of action, we can see all the ingredients of the Comedy of Action that we explored in the last chapter: an inflexible character in a situation that requires flexibility; characters driven by base needs such as greed; assumption; talking at cross-purposes; young lovers whose love has met challenges and the action operating within a specified time limit. These ingredients are in common with Menander, Goldoni and the television comedy of *Frasier,* for example. These are the elements which make up the popular contemporary stage comedies *Noises Off* and *One Man, Two Guvnors*.[4] However, although the mechanics of Plautus's plots are reminiscent of Menander, there are two new developments which make the Roman Comedy distinct from its Greek predecessor. The first development concerns character, and the second involves linguistic invention.

Plautus's characters hark back to the Attellan comedies, popular in Rome in the fourth-century BC. Euclio is a type of Manducus figure (a greedy clown); Megadorus is a type of Pappus (a doddery old man), and in the servants and slaves we can see the development of the Macchus (spiteful, and crafty while pretending to be stupid) and the Samnio (agile, stupid, fearful and hungry). However, Plautus also has his characters 'play against the mask'.[5] Euclio is not the type of miser who loves money for its own sake: he finds the pot of gold to be burdensome, and is relieved when he is legitimately poor at the end of the play. Eunomia may be full of advice, but she is not the familiar middle-aged scold. She shows compassion and nurture to her brother Megadorus and her son Lyconides. Megadorus is a reluctant suitor to Staphyla. He understands the practical benefits of marrying her, but is fully aware of how unlikely this is. He displays neither the vanity nor the arrogance that we might expect from the stock character of an elderly man.

There is a difference then to this comedy from the comedy that we examined in the previous chapter. We summarized the comedy of Menander, *Frasier* and *Curb Your Enthusiasm* as containing inflexible characters trapped in situations that demand flexibility. The plays of Terrance, Plautus and subsequently the comedy of Commedia dell'Arte involve characters who in some way embody a paradox. Robert S. Miola examines the convention of the *Miles gloriosus*, the braggart soldier.[6] In short the braggart soldier is the military man who will do anything to avoid actually fighting. As Miola explains, this figure is encountered throughout European theatre: the Italians usually make him Spanish and various Elizabethan writers (John Lily, Ben Johnson and Shakespeare) include this figure. Parolles in *All's Well that Ends Well* is a *miles gloriosus*.

Commedia dell'Arte is the form of theatre where we expect to meet comic characters. This sixteenth-century form features comic routines, songs, muddles and of course stock comic archetypes. Even though it may seem quite removed from contemporary theatre, television and film, we will discover that the archetypes that Commedia presents us are familiar. Harlequin, Pantalone, Brighella, Pulcinella are all stock characters who inhabit the stories. We are going to investigate them only briefly here – there are many sources available from which to learn the specifics of each of the characters, and their physical traits. Our interest in the characters is the role that they play in the narrative. We first meet the Brighella character in the comedy, *Epidicus*,[7] by Plautus. He has evolved by the time he recurs in the stories of the sixteenth-century Commedia, but his essence remains the same: a clever servant, masterful at manipulation and orchestration. In Commedia he is one of the Zanni – one of the servants at the bottom of the pecking order. As John Rudlin points out:

> Zanni is ignorant and loutish, and has no self-awareness. The very act of thinking is alien to him – the very sight of a Zanni straining to give birth to an idea is risible. But he is astute in knavery . . . intolerant of discipline and authority, but very faithful.[8]

Another of the zanni is the Harlequin. Originally, the Harlequin mask typified the stupid and ever-hungry servant, but he soon evolved into something more sophisticated:

> credulous and diffident, a lazy-bones but also a busybody, a mixture of cunning and ingenuousness, of awkwardness and grace.[9]

The Harlequin is a commentator both of the action onstage and of contemporary events offstage. We see this in the regular speeches directly addressed to the audience in Goldoni's plays. The Harlequin's main responsibility is to keep the comedy flowing. He is acrobatic, frenetic, sometimes frantic, mercurial and musical. Like Truffaldino in *A Master to Two Servants*, he is involved in, but at the same time somewhat peripheral to, the action – an observer who makes himself available to exploit the situation, but he does not have a direct effect on the events of the narrative. He is someone who reacts to action rather than initiates it.

The Pantalone is the old man who features in the plots of Commedia. We have already encountered him in the plays of Menander. He is often mean and avaricious, but at the same time a lover of finery. He is temperamental and often irritable; furious and quarrelsome. However, he can also be kind and benevolent. A Sicilian Abbot, Andrea Perrucci, writing about Commedia in the seventeenth century, points out:

> The avarice proper to old men is surpassed by an even greater vice, that of lust, unseemly in a person getting on in years.[10]

This brief description of these familiar comic characters reveals two essential facts about comedy:

1 Comedy depends to a certain extent on class.
2 Characterisation in comedy depends on the use of paradox.

In an earlier chapter, we have discussed the importance of tragedy occurring among an upper class. This is key to its effect on the audience. Comedy, on the other hand, depends on class distinction. In these stories, there are those who have an abundance of wealth, and those who have none. Generally speaking, the lower the status, the funnier the character. It is the poor and uneducated characters who seem to keep the comedy moving. This may appear a distasteful idea for these politically correct times, but it is even something that we teach our children from a young age, and is apparent in the cartoons that they watch. For over forty years, we have been enjoying *Scooby-Doo*[11] in its variety of incarnations. Eleven animated series, numerous feature-length animated films and four live-action films have shown us the enduring appeal of the type of class-based comedy similar to that of Menander, Plautus or Commedia dell'Arte. While *Scooby-Doo* is a mystery or 'whodunnit', its comedy trades on a fundamental archetype: Scooby and Shaggy (and in later series Scrappy-Doo) are zanni. They are blissfully unaware and lack self-criticism, their cowardice is apparent and their needs are base: 'Scooby snacks' and sleeping seem to be their priorities. Compared with Fred, Daphne and Velma, Scooby and Shaggy are uneducated and unsophisticated. While we look to Fred, Daphne and Velma to drive the plot, we look to Scooby and Shaggy to drive the comedy. Fred, Daphne and Velma also fit into a familiar pattern from Commedia: they are a different class from Shaggy and Scooby; they appear more wealthy and better groomed. Fred and Daphne are more attractive, and Velma is clearly more intelligent. They are reminiscent of the lovers and the doctor in a Commedia story. It is ironic, then, that Shaggy and Scooby are often left to confront the villain, and ultimately end up catching him as the result of some comic mishap.

These character types are recognisable in other cartoons also. *Top Cat*, *Hong Kong Phooey* and *Yogi Bear* are some of the other well-known cartoons that depend on characters at the bottom of the pecking order behaving like the archetypal zanni.

Once we recognize this comic archetype, we recognize them in other contexts. Sitcoms feature these characters often. Two zanni are clearly present in *Fawlty Towers*.[12] Polly is clearly recognisable as a Brighella character: clever, authoritative and resilient. Manuel is the second zanni, the Harlequin. He is the clown responsible for keeping the comedy moving: physically agile, uneducated, prone to misunderstandings and muddles, and only able to entertain one idea at a time. Manuel feels intensely, especially hunger, love and pain. This is also typical of the Harlequin. Together, Polly and Manuel come up with plots to deceive, or sometimes redeem, their boss, Basil Fawlty. While they are lower in status, they are somehow equal or better in fortune. They are a necessary team. Polly is quick in thought, and Manuel is quick in action, even if he does not necessarily understand exactly what is going on. Meanwhile Basil is a type of Pantalone: top of the pecking order, controlling of the finances, avaricious and grasping. Like any Pantalone, Basil Fawlty aspires to an old order, seeking approval from those he considers worthy. Much of the comedy in the episodes depends on the hotel not being the type of high-quality establishment that Basil would like it to be. They do not know how to make a 'Waldorf salad', there is a dead body in one of the rooms, and chef is indisposed before the first meeting of the prestigious supper club.[13] Basil is a Pantalone figure trying to keep control of a chaotic situation, and humiliation is the terrible price that he has to pay for not being able to keep control.

Paradox is the element that these Commedia characters have in common. The Brighella is lower in status than his (or her) master, but clearly more able and intelligent. The Pantalone aspires to attain status and wealth, but they evade him as his attempts become more desperate. The Harlequin is physically agile, but not mentally so quick. A decision made in the moment gets him into a situation without his realising the long-term implications. Paradox is key in creating a comic character. This use of paradox is similar to a plot device that we have previously discussed – the convergence of the incompatible. When the otherwise incompatible converge, comedy arises from the tension that is caused. For example, Dr Frasier Crane and his equally grand and aspiring brother Dr Niles Crane live with their ex-police officer father Martin and his English physiotherapist Daphne. The comedy often depends on these otherwise incompatible worlds colliding – worlds that are otherwise kept separate by class or social distinction. The brothers' sensibilities are compromised when they are forced to meet their father's work colleagues, or Daphne's eccentric working-class English family. The brothers are forced to suppress their surprise and horror, or even pretend to be something that they are not. There are many reported examples of the two brothers experiencing embarrassment during a visit to *Duke's*, their father's regular bar. Once again this comedy is dependent on diverse classes coming together. We could see the relationship between Fraser and Daphne and Martin as being similar to that between the Pantalone and the zanni – the control and status of the master converging with the chaos and mayhem of the servants. However paradox in character comedy has an additional layer: it is this convergence of the incompatible occurring within a person rather than within a situation – the dim-witted person of authority, the quick-witted person of low status.

This type of paradox is deeply satisfying to watch, as we come to recognize that there is paradox within us all. Identifying the paradox that is contained within can sometimes be an unwelcome exercise in self-reflection, but there are many linguistic clues as to how commonplace this paradox is – even though it may remain unrecognized. 'Inverted snobbery', 'champagne socialism', 'passive aggression', 'living death', 'the person we love to hate', 'method in their madness' – these are all common phrases that illustrate how we live with paradox daily. We respond to a character's paradox because we recognize its truth. However, from a technical perspective, paradox makes a character seem more believable and rounded. It means that they can be uncertain about something or make a surprising decision. The tension caused by the paradox within a character can be an effective source of drama or comedy. It gives the character something to push against and pull against, and it means that there can be surprises from an organic source rather than seeming contrived, or simply an example of the writer being 'clever'. The comedy in farce or sitcoms is not only based on the incompatible converging in the situation; the paradoxical and incompatible converges in the characters themselves.

Exercise

Invent characters that embody paradoxes. Write scenes or sketches in which the paradox comes to the fore. While these scenes may have many characters, only involve yourself with one character who embodies a paradox, otherwise it might become too complicated.

Exercise

Think about two different types of people who would be unlikely to meet in real life. Write a scene or a sketch in which they are forced together. What is the result of two pathologically incompatible characters converging?

Perhaps one of the most popular and enduring character-based television sitcoms is the US comedy *Friends*[14]. Paradox can be clearly located in each of the characters. Ross is the most academically accomplished of the group. He is a palaeontologist who teaches at a university, yet in his private life he behaves with a child-like, innocent quality, often needing quite straightforward things explained to him. If Ross is a foolish academic, then Phoebe is a wise fool: eccentric, idiosyncratic, flaky and forgetful. However she is often right about things. Her world view may be strange, but it is also strangely accurate. Rachel comes from a wealthy background, and has had everything provided for her by her parents throughout her life. After fleeing her own wedding, she finds herself in New York without an allowance and having to earn her own way; the rich young woman is suddenly penniless. Joey is uneducated and can appear dim, but he is good-natured and loyal. Despite this lack of intelligence, he plays a doctor in a long-running television series. It is interesting to note that both Ross and Joey have some sort of 'doctor' title, and both can be equally slow in understanding. There is an additional paradox involved with Joey: he is a reasonably well-known daytime soap actor who is clueless about acting. This leads to a complicated meta-textual paradox in the narrative. We are watching Matt LeBlanc playing Joey Tribbiani who in turn is playing Dr Drake Ramoray (badly). So, we have an actor who is acting an actor. Sometimes the scriptwriters seem to be having a great deal of fun with this; for example, in the episode in which Joey gives an acting lesson. Chandler is a brazen coward – perhaps a development of the *miles gloriosus*, the braggart soldier. He seems brazen, witty and confrontational, but at heart he is a coward. He spends most of the first series being intimidated by his girlfriend, Janice. Monica is a meticulous and accomplished chef, but no one wants to employ her. She is a cook with no one to cook for. She is highly competitive – unable to enjoy enjoyable activities, and also obsessively organized and tidy – a need to control an environment which, with her four friends, is otherwise uncontrollable. I would suggest that with its long-running plots about who is in love with whom, and all the complicated relationships, it almost resembles a long-running television drama. However, the paradoxes ensure heightened comic moments. The enduring appeal of *Friends* is watching these conflicted and paradoxical characters interact in situations that give rise to indecision, concealment and misunderstanding.

Another common element that we discern in comic characters is the notion of inflexibility. There is a certain lack of flexibility in the behaviour of the Crane brothers in *Frasier* or the characters in *Friends*. However, there are characters who are extreme with regard to this and extreme inflexibility gives rise to a type of paradox in itself. The character is rigid and inflexible, but the situation often demands flexibility, and through this paradox, a distinct type of comic character evolves: the monster. These characters lack self-awareness and they are inflexible to such a degree that the comedy becomes heightened and perhaps not to everyone's taste. Peter Sellers, John Cleese, Larry David, Ricky Gervais, and Sacha Baron Cohen are all adept at becoming comic monsters. They expose our taboos, and hypocrisies, and they transform into the embodiment of shameful and fearful elements of ourselves. The key to these characters is in how they are performed. They are performed without irony or self-consciousness, and the performer commits to the absolute truth of the imagination: they are inflexible, single-minded and monstrous.

Sacha Baron Cohen first came to public attention as the character Ali G.[15] Convinced that he is a black rapper and gang member (the West Staines Massif), Ali G is actually a suburban, middle-class white youth who lives with his grandmother. He is unable to perceive the world outside the parameters of his own narrow-minded delusions. Michael Edoba, editor of *New Nation*, commented on the character in an interview for The *Guardian*:

This character is rooted in a cultural phenomena of our times – namely that many young white and Asian youngsters adopt black personas [sic] and appear ridiculous to everyone besides themselves. I don't think that it is offensive.[16]

Baron Cohen then went on to create the character of Borat – a vulgar, sexist, anti-Semitic journalist from Kazakhstan whose bigoted views are used to expose the prejudice of Americans. His character Brüno is a gay Austrian fashion reporter who seems to believe that anything is acceptable in pursuit of fame. Admiral General Aladeen features in the film *The Dictator*,[17] whose strapline is 'the heroic story of a dictator who risked his life to ensure that democracy would never come to the country he so lovingly oppressed'. Note the oxymoron of 'lovingly oppressed' – indicative of the paradox involved in this type of comedy. Like the monstrous character of Lady Bracknell in *The Importance of Being Earnest*,[18] the key to these characters is that they adhere dogmatically to an (often paradoxical) idea with no concept that any other point of view is possible. Lady Bracknell believes no one to be her social equal. Inspector Clouseau understands nothing that is clear or obvious, even though he is leading an investigation into a stolen diamond. Ali G believes himself to be a black gang member, even though he is suburban and white. Borat is unable to discern what is publicly acceptable behaviour, even though as a presenter and journalist he is always operating publicly. To Brüno, anything is acceptable if in pursuit of fashion and image, and for the dictator Admiral General Aladeen, he is lost in America with a dictator's attitude, but no one to dictate to.

Exercise

Consider a paradox, and exploit it to create a monster. Write a scene in which flexibility is required, and the character has none. He or she is unable to assess what is demanded from the situation; taboos are broken and humiliation ensues.

This leads us to Aristotle's claim that comedy is 'an imitation of men worse than the average; worse, however, not as regards any and every kind of fault, but only as regards one particular kind, the ridiculous, which is a species of the ugly'.[19] Creating a monster involves concentrating on one particular kind of fault. The environment and the events of the story are all perceived through the filter of that one particular fault, and the monster acts and reacts accordingly. Like Elizabethan grammar school teachers using the plays of Terrence and Plautus to warn against the dangers of disobedience, lust and waywardness, the contemporary comic monster also serves to teach by example. Our own obsessive moments of inflexible madness – when we have refused to see the world through any other perspective – are made clear to us, lest we forget. The television critic Nancy Banks-Smith explains how a commitment to the seriousness elements of the monstrous can lead to comedy:

I strongly recommend you to have a look at tonight's episode when Tony Jordan, the Kohinoor in EastEnders' crown, writes a humorous Humpty Dumpty double act for this pair of slightly-past-their-prime porkers. When you have wrung the last drop of menace out of monsters, what remains like grains of gold is comedy.'[20]

Checklist

Here is a checklist if you wish to create your own characters based on these archetypes:

- Paradox is key. The character embodies paradoxical characteristics which are then exposed by the situation.
- Taboo breaking and shame are often a source of comedy in this context.
- There is comic potential in the convergence of the otherwise incompatible.
- The Commedia archetypes are still used in contemporary comedy.

8

HAPPILY EVER AFTER: ROMANTIC COMEDY FROM SHAKESPEARE TO *SLEEPLESS IN SEATTLE*

A union which leads to marriage or the coming together of life partners is a perilous adventure. It is this adventure that Romantic Comedy describes. In committing to a long-term relationship the stakes are high and in some historical periods (and even contemporary traditions), there is a sense of this choice being an 'once only' opportunity. In cultures that do not tolerate divorce or separation, there is no going back; the decision is inexorable. As we discovered early on in discussing the building blocks of story: choice and watching people make decisions is one of the key elements of constructing a story. So, in Romantic Comedy, we have people making a choice – which according to our romantic sensibilities and our traditions – we imagine that they are going to make only once in their lives. Making this choice is not straightforward. The entire story is consumed with making this one choice. The choice will finally be made as late in the narrative as possible and it will inevitably involve some sort of a muddle. In exploring Romantic Comedy, we will revisit other forms of comedy and see that essentially the structures and devices remain the same even though the context and order may be different. We will also discover that the romantic comedies we enjoy in the cinema and on stage today are still structured according to the basic principles which the Elizabethans (or even the Romans) understood over 400 (or 2,000) years ago.

Romantic Comedies must end with a union – two people committed to a life together, and then the narrative stops while we imagine that their life together continues happily. The structure is the same archetypal structure that we examined in earlier chapters:

$$\text{order} \rightarrow \text{chaos} \rightarrow \text{reorder}$$

Two people are in a routine, they meet, a muddle occurs, requited love is denied, but then eventually acknowledged, a commitment is made and a new order is established. The effect is that hope (or sentimentality) fills our hearts and then the story stops. As Graham Norton, the Irish comedian and television presenter puts it:

'movies end, books stop, songs finish but you've got to keep on going. And no one wants to think about the bickering at the end of *When Harry Met Sally*, or him fucking someone else. Why would they?'[1]

Therefore, like all comedy, timing is essential in Romantic Comedy. It is imperative that the denouement, and the union, occur at the last possible moment. The life of the characters once they are together is of no concern to us. We assume that they are going to lead perfect lives, and even if this is not our assumption, we are not interested in the banality of the couple's new life. We are intrigued by the mechanics of the union, and by the processes of choice and change, and how lives are reordered out of chaos.

Romantic Comedies reflect our need to idealize and romanticize relationships. They remain an immensely popular genre even though we know how the film or the play is going to end. The suspense is created by the 'how': how the union is going to occur; how the couple are going to overcome the muddle and achieve the clarity of vision that is necessary for them to realize that they are meant for each other. They help us to feel hopeful about the world by believing in the deep spiritual and emotional connection that happens between two people as if it were something preordained.

I suggest that the chaos that the characters endure, during the narrative, is an external manifestation of what we experience internally when we are embarking on a new relationship: the confusion, loss of identity and the sense of sacrifice that we encounter as an essential shift is occurring in our lives. This shift is one of perspective – from being at the centre of our own lives to putting someone else temporarily (or permanently) at the centre of our life. As love has its effect, our thoughts are busy with the new person: we imagine conversations we would like to have, or ways of surprising them and making them happy. This process seems to induce a particular type of neurosis. Falling in love, even when it is relatively trouble free, is a bewildering experience. As we experience a shift of focus from being the subject of our own lives to focusing on the object of our desire, the actions of another person exert an unreasonable and irrational force on us. Sometimes these feelings can be more intense than we are comfortable with and we experience something overwhelming: confusion, obsession, panic, loss, grief. This is what characters in Romantic Comedies endure, but the cause of these feelings – as we are dealing with plays and films, rather than novels or reality – has to be something external rather than internal. In Romantic Comedies, the confusion, loss and panic are a result of the visible mechanics of the narrative: the path of true love does not run smoothly. The obstacles that the characters must overcome must reflect the seriousness of the outcome – a union that is made only once in life, as two identities merge into one.

'Romantic love is an obsession. It possesses you. You lose your sense of self. You can't stop thinking about another human being.'[2]

The stakes must be high. The potential reward is great as are the risks: exclusion, abandonment, isolation and even sometimes death are possibilities, and will become acutely more real if the relationship is not realized. As a result, the element of comedy in this genre is often as painful as it is funny.

The nature of the muddle which prevents the easy transition into a union is generally one of three possibilities: concealed identity, a broken promise or a misunderstanding. For example, Shakespeare's *The Two Gentlemen of Verona* or *Twelfth Night*, or Hollywood films such as *Tootsie*[3] and *Some Like it Hot*[4] all involve someone concealing their true gender and falling in love while disguised as the opposite sex. This type of courtship brings about a unique circumstance which brings with it an unusual privilege. The possible tension caused by the unresolved sexual attraction is not apparent to one of the couple. The two people can communicate and get to know each other with a sense of equality and camaraderie unaffected by the rules of courtship. In *Twelfth Night,* Orsino explains to Viola, dressed as Cesario, that he has 'unclasped [to thee] the book even of my secret soul',[5] and later, he and Viola discuss what it means for a man to fall in love. Viola uses her privileged position to express a woman's view on how men love:

We men may say more, swear more, but indeed
Our shows are more than will, for still we prove
Much in our vows, but little in our love.[6]

This sense of intimacy is echoed in *Tootsie*. Michael dressed as Dorothy must share a bedroom with Julie while visiting her father Les. The room sharing happens because of Les' belief that that there is little point in their sleeping in separate rooms because as 'girls together' they will want to stay up all night and talk. The disguise allows Michael unprecedented access to the woman he loves. While Viola in *Twelfth Night* has gained privileged access to the man of her desires, Michael in *Tootsie* has taken the level of intimacy further; he has managed to share a bed with the woman he loves, albeit not romantically, and without her realising she is sharing a bed with a man. However, for both Viola and Michael, the disguise also brings with it a price. Both have the access and intimacy that they require, but they are prevented from declaring how they are feeling by the disguise they are forced to wear. The unresolved sexual tension is acute even though it is being experienced by only one of the pair. Perhaps the disguise in this genre has figurative parallels with our own real experience of courtship: once we discard our 'disguise' and confess our feelings there is no return to the safety of our otherwise concealed feelings. The real dilemma in our ritual of courtship is whether we should dispose of our disguise, and risk rejection, or continue enjoying access and intimacy but never really reveal our true self – a choice that in Romantic Comedy makes unspoken love and unrequited love so compelling.

Exercise

Consider a situation in which someone pretends to be someone else when meeting someone new. This need not necessarily involve cross-dressing. One of the pair falls in love with the other. Write three scenes:

1 The scene in which they fall in love

2 A scene in which one of the couple admits to a friend that they have fallen in love

3 The revelation – the disguised person reveals to the other person that he or she has been pretending to be someone else.

The muddle in Romantic Comedy does not necessarily involve disguise. A muddle might involve a love triangle, for example, and the suspense can then be sustained and the stakes remain high. The dramatic advantages of a love triangle are that a choice has to be made: someone will win, and someone will lose. Hopefully in a comedy, the loser is not the protagonist with whom we identify. In *Twelfth Night*, Shakespeare's skilful *deus ex machina* – the arrival of Sebastian, Viola's twin brother – solves one muddle, but creates another. It ensures that Olivia's loss is not at first apparent to her, and leads to a further muddle when a love triangle is created, and Orsino mistakes Sebastian for Viola's disguised alter-ego, Cesario. In *Tootsie*, Michael dressed as Dorothy causes an even more complex muddle. Not only does Dorothy manage to accrue two men as suitors, Les and John Van Horn, but also Michael leads Sandy to mistakenly think that he is in love with her while he is secretly in love with Julie who has no idea that he is really a man, as she only knows him as Dorothy. Several love triangles overlap. The feelings of loss and betrayal are somewhat softened in the moment of denouement by the comic impact of all of them simultaneously witnessing Dorothy revealing her disguise. This is a highly effective moment in the film: a montage of reactions as chaos is transformed into a new order through the truth being exposed – Dorothy taking off her disguise live on television as the soap is being transmitted and revealing that the actor playing her is really a man.

Exercise

Consider a plot which involves a love triangle. Write a scene involving all three people, but none of them is aware of the whole truth. How will you engineer the situation, so that the audience understand what is going on, but the characters remain unclear?

A broken promise can also be a cause of the muddle. *The Two Gentlemen of Verona*, *The Merchant of Venice*, *All's Well that Ends Well* all have plots which depend on a promise being broken in some way. There are several more contemporary cinematic examples of this plot device: the 1950s' romantic comedy, *Sabrina*,[7] the successful British comedy from the 1990s, *Four Weddings and a Funeral*,[8] and the twenty-first century comedy, *Crazy, Stupid, Love*,[9] all feature the muddle being caused by someone breaking a promise. A period of chaos then follows, before the character experiences a redemption of sorts, and realizes that commitment can lead to happiness. Of these numerous examples, *Sabrina* warrants closer examination, as it involves two potentially broken promises, neither of which is broken by the end of the story – leading to the redemption of the two male characters and the happiness of Audrey Hepburn's character, Sabrina.

Sabrina – played by Audrey Hepburn – is the daughter of a chauffeur who is employed by a wealthy family. She is in love with one of the sons, David Larrabee. David is a philanderer and we first meet him seducing a young woman at a party and arranging a secret rendezvous with her at the tennis courts with two glasses and a bottle of champagne. Sabrina witnesses this event on the night before she is to be sent to Paris to attend cookery college. The despair drives Sabrina to attempt to kill herself by inhaling the exhaust from the cars in her father's care, but she is saved by Linus, David's responsible, business-minded brother. Sabrina returns from Paris two years later transformed by her experience, and David immediately notices her and sets about repeating the seduction on the tennis courts – using the identical techniques that Sabrina had witnessed on that fateful day two years earlier. Linus prevents this meeting, as David is to marry the daughter of a businessman whose partnership is crucial in the family's new business venture. This dishonourable courting of Sabrina is the first potential broken promise of the film. While David is indisposed by an injury involving shards of champagne glass, Linus courts Sabrina in his place. As Linus continues to keep Sabrina occupied to protect his business interests and prevent her brother from breaking off his marriage, he begins to fall in love with her and she begins to develop feelings for him. Despite this he plans to keep her out of the way by asking her to show him Paris. He books two cabins on an ocean liner, and this is where the second broken promise is involved – he has no intention of joining her on board the ship. Sabrina discovers the plan, and the emotional and situational muddle intensifies until a last-minute resolve is reached: Linus changes his mind, and he and Sabrina are united on the ship. Linus honours his promise as a new relationship begins.

Committing to a promise, broken or otherwise, is a common device in Romantic Comedy. The commitment is representative of the wedding vows to come; the fulfilment of the promise in our story augurs well for the more serious promises required for a shared life in the future. Committing to a promise is the beginning of committing to a new relationship, a new alliance and a new life.

Incidentally, wooing *in loco*, as Linus does in *Sabrina*, seems to be an acceptable convention in Romantic Comedy. In *As You Like It*, Orlando woos Ganymede (Rosalind dressed as a boy) in order to practice wooing her in reality or perhaps cure him of his love. The story of *Cyrano de Bergerac*[10] in any of its manifestations involves Cyrano wooing Roxanne on behalf of Christian.

For the Elizabethans, like many cultures, marriage was as much a financial arrangement as it was a matter of love. It was often a way of securing a sustainable financial future for generations to come. In a culture which strongly disapproved of divorce or separation, this was a choice that could be made only once. The consequences of this choice would last a lifetime. Therefore, the dowry needed to be negotiated carefully like any business arrangement. The notion of a 'suitable match' is still something that might be important to us today. Even if the family background is less important, we might still consider several elements to be essential: a university degree, a good job, a respectable family, a history of good health, the potential to provide a stable income. This might be an indication as to the implication of Shakespeare's comedies involving disguise – a character is unable to reveal who they really are and so material considerations are removed. The disguise allows those involved to begin their relationship based on their personality and compatibility. The suitability of the union can to be explored without the pressure of background, class or wealth.

In *Twelfth Night*, Viola is in love with Orsino. She has dressed as a boy, in order to survive the homelessness of being stranded in a strange country following a shipwreck. She calls herself Cesario, and holds a position at Orsino's court. The muddle is made even more complex by Orsino – oblivious to Viola's true identity – using Viola to approach Olivia, the woman he is in love with. Olivia, in turn, falls in love with Viola dressed as Cesario, not knowing that he is really a young woman. As we have seen, Viola is able to get to know Orsino at court as a young woman never usually would; she is privy to witnessing him interact with him believing that he is in the company of men. There is a sense, therefore, that Viola's disguise allows her to experience Orsino undisguised – without the barriers necessitated by formal Elizabethan court traditions. Orsino and Viola represent an ideal but impossible courtship. She falls in love with him independent of the restraints of her family, while he establishes an intimate connection without the distraction that she is a young woman. Their initial connection is uncomplicated by class. It is convenient, then, that when she does reveal herself to him, she is a suitable match, and we know that her father has spoken favourably about Orsino.

It is the case in several of Shakespeare's plays that young women, unaware that they are royalty, are then wooed by young aristocratic men, and the marriage is allowed to take place because of the revelation that she is in fact from court. As we have seen, Rosalind is wooed in this way in *As You Like it*. Perdita is unaware of her heritage when she is courted by Florizel in *The Winter's Tale*. Ferdinand courts Miranda unaware of who she really is in *The Tempest*. In *Cymbeline*, it is the discovery of the lost princes that frees Imogen from the pressures of succession and makes her free to marry Posthumus. Perhaps this device of disguise serves not only to create a muddle, and to allow characters the freedom to court free of their identity, but also to restore our faith that the choice we make is based on a romantic basis rather than a material one. We are reassured that true love does indeed win through.

Exercise

Consider a situation in which two people may get to know each other without really knowing each other's status or financial situation. Write the scene in which they first get to know each other. How can you engineer a situation which guarantees a type of anonymity for the characters. What freedom does it give to the beginning of the relationship? How do the characters interact without status and class being an issue?

The development of the relationships in Elizabethan Romantic Comedy follows a path which reflects the process of courtship and marriage in England before the reforms. The first stage in the plays is the recognition of the attraction. This is usually quite a private matter, and is revealed either to another character or directly to the audience in a soliloquy. The second stage is the exchanging of rings. Finally there is the marriage or the public commitment to vows of future marriage. The events in some of the plays involve restoring the order to this process when it has become disordered. In *The Taming of the Shrew*, for example, the marriage occurs without Kate's consent, but by the end of the play she publicly expresses her commitment to Petruchio. This public commitment is essential in restoring propriety to the ritual. In *All's Well that Ends Well*, Helena must engineer the exchange of rings by deceit in order to make Bertram agree to go through with the public ceremony. This is also true of Marianna and Angelo in *Measure for Measure*. In *The Merchant of Venice*, the rings are exchanged, but then given away. In *Twelfth Night*, Viola unwittingly accepts a ring from Olivia under the pretence that she had left it behind. In *Much Ado About Nothing*, Claudio leaves the wooing of Hero to a masked Don Pedro, but the union only successfully goes ahead when, thinking her to be dead, he publicly announces his love for her. In the act of repentance, he now verbally commits to her. It seems, then, that many of Shakespeare's comedies are concerned with restoring order to the process of courtship once this process has in some way been derailed.

Contemporary romantic comedies operate slightly differently from Elizabethan ones, but there is still a distinct order that needs to be adhered to and many are all still concerned with a process of courtship which has been disturbed.[11] The moment of recognition is still key, and this moment in which each person realizes that they have fallen in love must be evident. This is not necessarily done with a monologue or soliloquy, but with recognisable camera work: soft focus and lingering looks, so that the moment of falling in love can also be located. In *Tootsie*, Michael realizes that he is in love with Julie when he sees her being treated badly by her director boyfriend. Listening to his stories of a past broken heart makes Sabrina fall for Linus. This recognisable turning point is often followed by a confession to a close friend in order to establish for the audience the way the character feels. However, in a film romantic comedy, the couple remain either ignorant of each other's feelings or uncommitted to the relationship until the very end. Here then are the stages of development in contemporary Romantic Comedies:

- The characters are established – we learn about who they are and the world they inhabit
- The couple encounter each other, but it is clear that they are not compatible and a relationship is unlikely.
- A moment occurs in which one of the characters falls in love.
- A broken promise, a disguise or a misunderstanding causes a muddle to ensue.
- The muddle intensifies so that it appears to be unsolvable.
- A confession or quirk of fate leads to a last-minute union.

Shakespeare's Romantic Comedies all seem to involve three separate classes or worlds which then converge at various points in the story. *Much Ado About Nothing* involves the world of the soldiers, the world of Leonato's court and the world of the constables. The action during *Twelfth Night* takes place in Orsino's court, in Olivia's court and among the comic aristocracy of Sir Toby, Sir Andrew and Maria. There may be convergences and cross-referencing, but the worlds are essentially distinct until they inevitably collide at the end of the play. This structure of three separate worlds coexisting is not uncommon in contemporary film versions of the Romantic Comedy. *Crazy, Stupid, Love*,[12] for example, features the marriage of Cal and Emily which requires healing, the romance between Jacob and Hannah which requires parental consent, and the friendship between Jessica and Robbie which requires clarification. The middle-aged couple, the young couple and the teenagers essentially inhabit different worlds, but it is the convergence of these three worlds and the various muddles caused by the story's initial broken promise which drives the narrative. While this element of three worlds converging is not a necessary device for Romantic Comedy, *Crazy, Stupid, Love, Tootsie*, *When Harry Met Sally* and *Sabrina* all involve three separate worlds intersecting. Both in Shakespeare's writing and in contemporary film, this gives the story a broader and more inclusive context, presenting us with what we imagine is a more complete universe. In the contemporary setting, it also shows relationships blossoming from people who would normally not be considered compatible as they come from different worlds. Perhaps this gives us a feeling of hope that love in this romantic context can transcend barriers, or perhaps it might illustrate – as Helen Fisher suggests – that we are designed to seek love from as far outside our gene pool as possible. We fall in love regardless of our status, class or demographic. This fills us with hope – something this particular genre is designed to do:

> There's all kinds of reasons that you fall in love with one person rather than another. Timing is important. Proximity is important. Mystery is important. You fall in love with somebody who's somewhat mysterious, in part because mystery elevates dopamine in the brain. Probably pushes you over that threshold to fall in love.[13]

In *Much Ado about Nothing*, Beatrice asks Benedict to 'kill Claudio'. This gives us some indication of a theme often explored in Romantic Comedy: allegiance. As we enter the emotional chaos which falling in love and courtship involves, we are entering into a process that involves allegiances shifting. A new person is becoming the priority over self, family, friends or professional responsibilities. This echoes a biblical idea about the shift in priority which marriage entails:

> Therefore a man will leave his father and his mother and cleave unto his wife; and they shall be one flesh.[14]

When Beatrice asks Benedict to kill Claudio, she is asking for a new allegiance to be formed. He will be allied to a new world – the women of Leonato's court – rather than his old world, the allegiances necessary for soldiers at war. This shift in loyalty is not to be underestimated; Benedict's allegiance to Claudio would have been a matter of life and death on the battlefield. They would have depended on each other for support, safety, companionship and brotherly love. He is being asked to sacrifice this relationship and ally himself with a new group. He is being challenged to develop a new sense of loyalty which he regretfully agrees to do. There is a scene in *When Harry Met Sally*[15] in which Marie and Jess are moving in together, and she is saying which of his artefacts may be taken into their new home and which of them are to be thrown away. In a way, this is an example of forging a new allegiance. Jess is abandoning the tastes of his past, and reluctantly embracing the aesthetic of his new partner. *Sleepless in Seattle*[16] involves Annie's allegiance with Walter coming to an end, as she forms a new allegiance with someone she has never met before, and whose voice she has heard only on the radio.

Checklist

Here is a checklist if you would like to use the model of Romantic Comedy in your writing:

- A couple (or couples) meet, but owing to some sort of muddle they are unable to admit they are in love with each other until the very end of the narrative.
- The muddle will involve concealment, disguise, a broken promise or a misunderstanding.
- There may be three different worlds included in the narrative.
- There will be a sense of each of the couple switching allegiance, and this will be a confusing process.
- The moment of falling in love must be acknowledged in the narrative.
- There will be a sense of the relationship being stronger because it has survived a sequence of tests.
- Often the narrative involves trying to get the process of courtship in the correct order: meeting, acknowledging love, promise of love, commitment to the relationship.
- The narrative ends following the commitment to a relationship.

9

MINDING OUR MANNERS: *THE COUNTRY WIFE* AND *MEAN GIRLS*

As we enter into our fourth and final comedy genre, you might question why this is not simply a subgenre of Romantic Comedy, which it so often resembles, and why it deserves a chapter of its own. Even though the plots of Comedy of Manners might at times seem familiar, and at the end a union occurs, the driving force behind the comedy is distinctly different. The purpose is not to reassure us of the value of true love, or that love will conquer adversity as a new life begins. The impulse behind Comedy of Manners is perhaps more cynical and critical. This genre arises out of the need to defeat oppression, and set the spirit free. Restoration Comedy of the eighteenth century is a response to the preceding rule of Cromwell's Puritan Interregnum in which the public theatres were closed. The main impulse behind this genre of comedy is to expose hypocrisy, whether we are dealing with the Restoration comedies of William Wycherley or John Vanbrugh, for example, or the comedies of Oscar Wilde or Noël Coward. Even in contemporary films such as *Mean Girls*,[1] *Clueless*[2] or *Legally Blonde*,[3] an institution is being criticized, and the Romantic Comedy plot becomes almost incidental. The institution under fire might be class, or bureaucracy or celebrity. The point is that the element which deserves satirising has become so inflated that it is no longer operating within reason. The joy in watching a Comedy of Manners is in watching a type of madness being exposed. As Nietzsche clarifies:

> Madness is rare in individuals, but in groups, parties, nations and ages it is the rule.[4]

This is the function of this type of comedy. It examines the conventions that we construct, and pokes fun at how ridiculous they are. It is an opportunity to knock the establishment, the conservative or the authoritative and provoke a change in behaviour and beliefs. The satirical nature of the comedy is of equal importance to the plot. In fact, in many Comedies of Manners the plots often seem hurried or even flawed. John Vanbrugh, the Restoration playwright, admits:

> The chief entertainment, as well as the moral, lies much more in the characters and dialogue than in the business and the event.

The key to working with this genre is locating the truth in the context being examined, and magnifying the element of truth to make it appear ridiculous. The comedy must begin with something that the audience recognizes as authentic. The temptation is to contrive the mockery before there is a real basis for criticism. The result of this is that the comedy is simply camp. Before the notion of 'camp' meant overtly theatrical, or flamboyant, or before it became a ready shorthand for homosexual, it had a much more specific meaning. I suggest 'camp' in its purest form means the emphasis on *form* rather than *content*. 'Camp' is the preoccupation with how something is said rather than what is being said, so manner becomes more prevalent than anything else. Of course the result might be something overtly theatrical or flamboyant, but this concept of form being more important than content is a useful one. This is the danger lurking when writing, acting in or directing a Comedy of Manners: the wit may be skilful, acerbic or cutting, but unless it is justified, by offering analysis of something worth criticising, it simply comes across as futile or even a little nasty. This is why this type of comedy is so suitable for exposing hypocrisy – hypocritical behaviour is a fair target for critical humour, especially when this behaviour is that of the establishment, or those representing authority. The British actor Simon Callow points out the danger of performing in a Restoration Comedy – what happens when the content of what is said becomes lost to the manner in which it is said, and the performance simply becomes camp:

> If the audience loses the sense of what's being said, then the plays can seem like a lot of people archly posturing together. It's a waste of the rich red meat of these texts.[5]

The heightening of manner and situation in the writing and performing is essential, but this brings with it dangers. If the heightening happens without any truth, then we are left with something full of affectation and irrelevance. Connecting with something truthful is key to understanding the mechanics of Comedy of Manners. The stories may seem to be about posturing, self-presentation and nuanced behaviour, but the comedy drawn from this only has value if something more substantial is being satirized.

Perhaps this is the mistake made by many current British and American television situation comedies. The targets of the humour seem somewhat indiscriminate, and not always justified, which can make the humour appear nihilistic, or even spiteful. There is little point attacking the downtrodden, the oppressed or those who are genuinely doing good (or at least not doing any harm). US television and film are currently experiencing a renaissance in this form of comedy. There are some effective examples of Comedy of Manners being produced, such as the films *Clueless, Mean Girls* and *Legally Blonde*, and the television series *Parks and Recreation*,[6] *30 Rock*[7] and *Community*.[8] Each of these is very clear about the elements of American society that are being criticized: snobbery, institutionalized stupidity, the undeserving rich and bureaucracy.

Perhaps we sometimes struggle to find a relevant context in which to set a Comedy of Manners. The setting is essential to the comedy's success. The Restoration Comedies of the seventeenth century were an expression of freedom. Released from the oppressive Puritan government of Cromwell, the theatres could once again be open; flamboyance, opulence and liberalism could be celebrated. Men and women could be seen to dress to impress, and be seen to show off their wealth and attractiveness. The topics of the plays could be courtship, relationships and sex without there being any fear of reprisal because King Charles II was so enamoured of the theatre, its spectacle and its actresses. It seems that throughout history, a clue to how urgently the need for liberation is felt is in the hairstyle; whether the 1960s, the 1980s or the late seventeenth century, fashionably long hair, especially in men (and short hair in women), is indicative of a need to break free. Restoration Comedy is known for men wearing extravagant wigs.

Key to the efficacy of the context in which the stories are set is the notion that there is something unspoken, something that still must remain concealed: promiscuity, identity, intelligence, authenticity – a rift between what can be said in public and what is the private truth. Shame is the 'sword of Damocles' which hangs over the heads of the characters. Often, this sense of shame is about not appearing to have worth in society's view. It might even be linked to sexual behaviour: the women might be immodest, and the men might be cuckolded. If elements of the private world are revealed in a more public arena, then shame is the inevitable result. Shame is such a powerful motivating force, and is instantly understandable and emotive for an audience watching. However, as we will see, there is one character who is impervious to shame, the fop. He (or more recently she) is sufficiently self-obsessed to be oblivious to ridicule or embarrassment. This, then, is a source of immense, but painful, enjoyment. It is significant that successful contemporary comedies of this type have a specific setting: an office, or the world of high fashion, or specific areas of California – places where reputation and appearances are important and potential shame is always looming.

Exercise

Consider an environment which, in your view, supports hypocrisy, or where form is more important than content. For example, this might be within a certain group at a college, or in the world of fashion or media. Write a scene in which the behaviour expected in this environment, the codes and mores, are clear to the audience. There is no need to be satirical at this stage – simply make the values of the environment you are writing about clear, and illustrate the potential for shame.

Let us begin by looking at William Wycherley's seventeenth-century comedy *The Country Wife*.[9] This is an example of one of the many comedies which was written following the Restoration of the Monarchy in 1660. It is celebratory of the sensual pleasures enjoyed by the aristocracy and critical of the middle-class puritanism which was associated with Oliver Cromwell's Commonwealth. This is the first time that women are permitted to act in London, and so the sparring between the sexes takes on a new vibrancy. This comedy, like so many comedies of this type, begins with an arrival. Pinchwife has married a young woman from the country, thinking that her unsophisticated tastes will keep his fortune and his reputation safe. The new wife is innocent to the ways of the city, and needs to have certain things explained to her by Pinchwife's sister, Alithea:

Alithea: Where? Would you have me civil? Answer 'em in a box at the plays, in the drawing room at Whitehall, in St James's Park, Mulberry Garden, or –

Pinchwife: Hold, Hold! Do not teach my wife where the men are to be found! I believe that she's the worse for your town documents already. I bid you keep her in ignorance, as I do.[10]

The films, *Clueless* and *Mean Girls,* and the very first episode of the UK version of *The Office*[11] all begin with the arrival of a newcomer who does not understand the conventions of their new environment, and needs the situation explained to them. Both the scenes in each of the two films are remarkably similar. Tai has come to Los Angeles from New York in *Clueless* and in *Mean Girls*, Cady has come to Los Angeles from Africa where her parents have been working. The similar scene involves the landscape of the school being mapped out to each newcomer according to which group sits where.

Whether a Restoration Comedy or a high-school comedy, the reason for this similarity in beginning these narratives – over 300 years apart – is clear: we, the audience, need to comprehend the way the environment works in order for us to understand exactly what hypocrisies are being exposed. In the same way that the rules of the *game* are explained in the first instance in Comedy of Action in order for us to understand the plot, we need to understand the environment of a Comedy of Manners in order to appreciate immediately what is being satirized.

Exercise

Consider the environment from the previous exercise. Introduce a newcomer who is unfamiliar to this world. Write a scene in which the codes of behaviour are explained to them, and the different types of character that they might meet.

The plot of Wycherley's *The Country Wife* has three interweaving strands: Pinchwife's attempts to keep his wife from corruption, Horner's plot to declare himself impotent so that he can meet with the wives of local businessmen without their suspicion and the courtship of Harcourt and Alithea. *The Country Wife* perhaps owes more to the comedies of Molière and the Roman writers, Terence and Plautus, than most comedies in this genre – some of which do not even offer a resolution for the plot. It is a neat and balanced three-strand structure in form. Scattered throughout the plot are the comic set pieces – sketch-like scenes which serve to satirize the hypocrisy of the middle classes and their attitude to morality, while celebrating the upper classes who are so blatantly liberated.

   In the characters of Sparkish and Horner, we meet the fop and the rake. We meet these characters again and again in Comedy of Manners. As the form evolves they develop and even sometimes merge, but they remain present in some form or another in all manifestations of this comedy. The character of the rake is dealt with simply: the man with the reputation for promiscuity and sexual appetite. We meet this type of comic character often, whether Horner in *The Country Wife*, or Joey Tribiani in *Friends*. Perhaps our politically correct times have caused this type to become subverted, so that we more frequently encounter the reformed rake (the womanizer who is trying to lead a better life), or like Joey Tribiani, the unsuccessful rake. The fop is a more complex figure. He is perhaps more commonly known as a dandy. He is concerned with appearance, manner, fashion and wit. There seems to have been some confusion in the twentieth century concerning the sexual orientation of the fop. In Restoration Comedy, there is no indication that the fop is a homosexual:

> Fops are narcissists, not homosexuals. They pursue women enthusiastically, their vanity protecting them from any mockery their efforts receive.[12]

In *The Country Wife*, Sparkish values dining with the other wits, but more than this, he values being seen in public at the theatre on the first night of a play:

> Pshaw! With you fooling we shall lose the new play. And I would no more miss seeing a new play the first day than I would miss sitting in the wits' row. Therefore I'll fetch my mistress and away.[13]

The fop, then, is consumed by the superficial; vain, loquacious and posturing. As Dorilant explains:

> No, he can no more think the men laugh at him than that the women jilt him, his opinion of himself is so good.[14]

In a later Restoration Comedy, John Vanbrugh creates an even more extravagant fop, the aptly named Lord Foppington, in the play *The Relapse*. This character makes his first appearance in Colley Cibber's comedy *Love's Last Shift*. In this play he has not become a lord yet, and is known as Sir Novelty Fashion. Already in this play, he is such an extravagant character that he wears a wig so big he is unable to walk, and has to be carried on stage in a sedan chair. By the time he reappears in Vanbrugh's play, he has morphed – along with his new title – into arguably one of the most exaggerated and flamboyant characters in all of Restoration Comedy. Let us take this example of his explanation of his daily routine:

> I rise madam, about ten o'clock. I don't rise sooner, because 'tis the worst thing in the world for the complexion; nat that I pretend to be a beau; but a man must endeavour to look wholesome, lest he be compelled to turn their eyes upon the play. So at ten a-clack, I say, I rise. Naw, if I find 'tis a good day, I resalve to take a turn in the Park, and see the fine women; so huddle on my clothes and get dressed by one. If it be nasty weather, I take a turn in the chocolate-hause: where as you walk, madam, you have the prettiest prospect in all the world; you have looking-glasses all round you.[15]

Lord Foppington is a man who cannot imagine that someone might want to go to the theatre to look at a play rather than look at him, or that you would not want to spend time looking at your own reflection in a chocolate house. It is interesting to note the use of language. Even Lord Foppington's speech has an affectation: the o's are turned into a's. This is further evidence that how something is said is more important than what is said. Form is more important than content.

What is interesting about the character of the fop is when he is exaggerated to the point of becoming almost monstrous. The degree of self-interest or conceit can become so overwhelming that the audience's response is one of shock, horror and delight. When the characterisation is both monstrous and also is recognisable as truthful, then the comedy is highly effective. Apart from Restoration Drama, we meet various fops in the plays of Oscar Wilde and Noël Coward, but we are also familiar with other iconic fops in our culture. The 'foppishness' is not dependent on any sexual orientation. In real life, both the football player David Beckham and the singer Elton John are fops. In fiction, the fop also exists across genres: James Bond (as portrayed by Sean Connery or Roger Moore, rather than the Daniel Craig incarnation) is a fop; Michael Douglas portrays the character of Liberace as a recognisable and flamboyant foppish character in the biopic *Behind the Candelabra*;[16] Alan Partridge[17] is a fop. We can see, then, that when identified as someone extravagant, self-involved, more interested in form than content, this foppish character's range is as diverse as the context in which he can be found.

Contemporary television situation comedies celebrate the comic potential of the fop. I would argue that *The Office*, *Parks and Recreation* and *Community* all contain a modern manifestation of the fop. David Brent, Leslie Knope and Jeff Winger all display similar attributes – they are self-interested, ambitious, have somewhat over-inflated egos and consider style more important than substance. Jeff Winger, in the first episode of *Community*, even admits:

> I discovered at a very early age that if I talk long enough, I can make anything right or wrong. So either I'm God or truth is relative. In either case, booyah!

Perhaps one of the joys of the fop's behaviour is in watching someone who is so uncritical of their own self-importance. We might all secretly be envious of this quality, wishing that we could act in such a way – a way that is frankly unacceptable in anyone over the age of about three. There is something liberating about this. By enjoying this type of character, we are in some way setting ourselves free.

Despite the fop's extravagance and sense of self-importance, there is another element to him that we enjoy – his playful use of language. As we can see from the above quotation from *The Relapse*, there is a great deal of fun in Lord Foppington's need to embellish and elongate vowel sounds. We come to expect this idiosyncrasy and we laugh anew each time our expectation is fulfilled. We still delight in this playfulness with language. In the film, *Mean Girls*, there is a character called Gretchen Wieners. Already her name indicates that she is a comic character. She is one of the 'plastics' and Regina's sidekick. This particular group of young women operate according to a code of inclusion and exclusion – a perfect context for a Comedy of Manners. There is also a linguistic element to this code – phrases that they repeat and signify that they belong to this cool group.

> **Regina:** We do not have a clique problem at this school.
> **Gretchen:** But you have to watch out for 'frenemies'.
> **Regina:** What are 'frenemies'?
> **Gretchen:** 'Frenemies' are enemies who act like friends. We call them 'frenemies'.

What makes Gretchen such an interesting character is that even though she is a relatively low-status character in the group, she is trying to empower herself through language. She is unsuccessfully trying to introduce the word, 'fetch' into their culture. This word is meaningless to everyone, but Gretchen is persistent.

> **Gretchen:** That is so fetch!
> **Regina:** Gretchen, stop trying to make fetch happen! It's not going to happen!
> **Gretchen:** That was so fetch!

On another occasion, Gretchen tries to justify her use of the word, by saying 'Oh, it's like slang, from . . . England.' In this world of style over substance, in which foppery is rewarded, Gretchen's only way of competing with the other members of the clique is to show dominance linguistically. We enjoy her successes, but we especially enjoy her failures.

Exercise

Consider how a fop might fit into the world that you made up for the previous two exercises. Write a scene involving this character. The degree to which he (or she) is monstrous is up to you. They also do not need to have a linguistic affectation. However they are vain, self-interested and immune to criticism. How do they interact with other characters?

This linguistic enjoyment is also seen in the use of repartee. The notion of repartee has perhaps become a little unfashionable; there is not an abundance of contemporary examples. The distinction between wit and repartee is clear. Wit is verbal ingenuity, especially for 'the ability to discover brilliant, surprising and paradoxical figures of speech'.[18] Repartee is a term taken from fencing, to mean a contest of wit, 'in which each person tries to cap the remark of the other or to turn it to his or her own purpose'.[19] In Shakespeare's *Much Ado about Nothing*, we have the banter of Beatrice and Benedick which seems to centre around a feeling of loss or even betrayal; in William Congreve's *The Way of the World*,[20] there is Mirabell and Millamant discussing their wedding. This banter is not quite the same as Ross and Rachel in *Friends*[21] or Nick and Jess in *New Girl*.[22] The repartee is a competition of wit, the significance of which is understood and enjoyed by both participants. In Restoration Comedy, women are seen on stage for the first time, so this competition of verbal prowess takes on a new significance. The battle of the sexes is being played out for the first time in British theatre between a man and a woman. It is fast moving, sometimes acerbic, sometimes vulgar. Often the woman is seen to win. It is clear that both understand the transaction which is occurring through topping the other's witticism or trading insults and both seem to enjoy it. In comparison, the banter of contemporary sitcoms seems sentimental. There is a sense that one (or both) of the characters is a victim, and there is not enough self-conscious joy in the quality of the exchange. The enjoyment in exchanging witty comments or insults is caused by the fact that both remain invulnerable. They can compete but at the same time conceal the true nature of the banter; both can flirt, but no one has to overtly reveal how they are really feeling, and in doing so, risk rejection.

Exercise

Two characters are attracted to each other, but for many reasons they are unable to admit it. Write a scene in which these characters have a conversation, and they want to talk about the one thing that they are not willing to broach: how much they like each other. How quickly does the scene become about frustration? How willing are they to insult each other? How do they make it clear that these insults are not real? Do they enjoy the insulting nature of the banter?

When looking at action comedy, we encountered the 'lazzi' – a pause in the action for some comic business, a sketch-like scene whose purpose is often to distract from the plot. Comedy of Manners has its own version of this. As a Comedy of Manners involves the introduction of a newcomer to a particular world, the sketch-like scene concerns how to do something. In Congreve's *Way of the World*, we have a scene involving the intricacies of holding a fan. In *Legally Blonde*, there is a scene about how to attract a man by picking up an object in a particular way, the 'bend and snap'. As Maurice observes when he walks in on the women practicing, 'Oh my God, the bend and snap works every time!'

Exercise

Write a scene in which someone is taught some way of behaving that brings about an effective result. This is a stand-alone scene, and does not require a connection to any plot elements. The comedy works best if there is some truth in the code of behaviour that is being shown.

Restoration Comedy develops into Sentimental Comedy once Charles II's reign ends, and the monarchy becomes more conservative. The flamboyance remains but there is an underlying moral message contained in the narrative. Essentially, this is the Comedy of Manners we are used to today. The narrative may seem risqué, or taboo breaking, but there is an inherent morality to the story. As Oliver Goldsmith explains:

> The virtues of private life are exhibited rather than the vices exposed, and the distresses rather than the faults of mankind make our interest in the piece.[23]

This is what we encounter in many of today's comedies; despite the follies of the characters, they are essentially good people. The films of Christopher Guest are a case in point. The characters may be foolish or pursuing a goal in a comically single-minded way, but they are always portrayed with compassion, and a sense that they are valuable as human beings.

Discussing the films of Christopher Guest leads us on to look at the 'mockumentary' as a worthy successor to Restoration Comedy in the lineage of Comedy of Manners. *The Office*, *Parks and Recreation*, *Community*, *Waiting for Guffman* and *Best in Show* are all mock documentaries which ask us to take a good look at the behaviour in specific, almost rarefied, environments. By examining the paradoxes and hypocrisies of these characters, we then laugh in recognition at our own behaviour. The fourth wall is often broken in Comedy of Manners, as a character turns to the audience and makes an aside. The self-conscious documentary context allows characters to do the same. David Brent in *The Office* or Leslie Knope in *Parks and Recreation* will often just glance long enough at the camera to make us jump. The effect of this is perhaps counter-intuitive; we might expect that we are becoming aware of the fiction that is the story, and therefore disengage, but actually we feel more included by this direct address and we are willing to become more involved. The other characters are almost excluded at this moment – their ridiculousness is highlighted while we share something intimate with one of the people in the story.

Checklist

Here is a checklist if you wish to write a piece inspired by Comedy of Manners:

- Set the story in an environment in which appearance, codes of behaviour and merit are all important. Shame is an important factor in this.
- A newcomer arrives, and the way the world works is explained to them.
- Plot is less important than exposing the hypocrisies of the characters in this particular environment.
- Include a fop. This person is consumed with self-interest and vanity. Their sense of self is almost impenetrable.
- Include a 'lazzi' – a stand-alone episode in which a particular way of behaving is explored.
- Include repartee or banter between two characters who are attracted to each other.
- For the plot, use a diluted form of Romantic Comedy or Comedy of Action.
- Inclusion and exclusion are the currencies of this world.
- If you are writing a 'mockumentary', allow the characters to be aware of the camera.
- Use three different strands of plot which interweave with one another. Like a Comedy of Action or a Romantic Comedy, each strand uses our two plot constructions:

$$\text{order} \rightarrow \text{chaos} \rightarrow \text{reorder}$$

and

$$\text{choice} \rightarrow \text{consequence} \rightarrow \text{change}$$

10
NOTHING EVER HAPPENS: CHEKHOV AND THE CONTEMPORARY INDEPENDENT COMEDY

A light-hearted way of looking at this type of narrative might be to say that there are three phases to a Chekhov play:

- Nothing happens
- Nothing happens
- Something happens and nothing is ever the same again.

Chekhov implies something similar:

> Let us be just as complex and as simple as life itself. People dine and at the same time their happiness is made or their lives are broken.[1]

The juxtaposition of the banal and the life-changing makes for a powerful form of narrative, which is widely used. It is a form common to contemporary theatre and film.

Let us begin with a play which predates Chekov's work: Turgenev's *A Month in the Country*.[2] This is a play involving a changing Russia, the experience of paralysis and the inability to change. The need for industry and the construction of a new Russia is juxtaposed with extreme boredom and inertia. One consequence of this unhappy mix is jealousy of youth and the destruction of a young woman's hope for her future happiness. Natalya Petrovna lives with her husband, son and her seventeen-year-old ward on a rural estate. She spends the days idly passing the time with her admirer Rakitin while her husband Islayev is busy improving the lives of those living on his land. Both Natalya and her ward, Vera, fall in love with the tutor, Belyaev. In an act of jealousy, Natalya has Vera marry the older neighbour, Bolshintsov – forcing Vera to have the kind of marriage with an older man that she herself has had to endure. Belyaev sees Natalya's confession of love for him as a political victory in that he is finally in a position of power over the land-owning classes. Generations of oppression experienced by his ancestors are resolved in this one event, and he is hopeful for the new Russia. Belyaev leaves the estate and Natalya is left alone; abandoned by those she once relied on for company. Her husband continues with his work, making the lives of those living on his land better. He is oblivious of this private turmoil which has been occurring on his estate. The reordering of Russia's political landscape is reflected in the reordering in the personal lives of each of the main characters.

We can already see in this story many of the signature elements of a Chekhov play: a tension between the old way and the new; hope dissolving; and the victory of political idealism. Boredom is the impulse which drives the narrative. This may seem like a counter-intuitive idea, but there is a great deal about boredom that is dramatic. When people are experiencing boredom they begin to do interesting – albeit destructive – activities: gossiping, arguing, fighting, falling in love, hatching plans. The important element when putting people in a setting with nothing to do is to get the right mix of people. Chekhov was skilled at this. In *The Cherry Orchard*,[3] for example, we witness a bankrupt matriarch and her elderly brother, a clever businessman, an idealistic student, an adopted daughter, her actual daughter, a vaudeville performer and a variety of other neighbours and staff. By trapping these diverse characters in the one location, drama inevitably ensues. It is also significant that in the case of Chekhov, these places are extremely remote, so the characters are geographically forced to remain together.

This model is repeated in contemporary plays and film. *Jerusalem*,[4] *Tribes*,[5] *Choir Boy*,[6] *The Ice Storm*,[7] *The Big Chill*,[8] *The Royal Tennenbaums*,[9] *Margot at the Wedding*[10] and many of Woody Allen's films are all examples of stories that employ this device – the convergence and entrapment of the pathologically incompatible. Even though some of the examples above involve an urban setting, there is still a sense of the characters being stuck together and untangling themselves emotionally is the last resort. The films of Woody Allen and Wes Anderson create this feeling. It goes without saying that this convergence is a useful device for writing for theatre – it requires only one location. In a previous chapter on comedy, we noted that there is much value to be had with the structure of the pathologically incompatible converging in a certain place at a certain time. This is also true for this genre, and it serves to remind us that these plays and films are linked to comedy in terms of their heritage. It has been observed that the characters converging fit into one of two categories – residents and outsiders.[11] There are those who belong to the environment permanently, and those who are just passing through, even if the passing through takes several years – as is the case of the officers in *Three Sisters*.[12] The tension between the residents and the outsiders creates a fundamental incompatibility – one that requires the events of the play to resolve.

Exercise

Consider a situation which sees a variety of characters forced to converge, and then remain together. The location is remote, and there is no way of contacting anyone outside the group. There is nothing to do, and monotony ensues. If you wish, make a distinction between those characters who are residents and those who are outsiders. Write a scene exploring what might happen under these circumstances. It is important to know precisely who the characters are. What is the source of the drama? To what heights can you take this drama?

The paradox about these stories is that although nothing seems to happen, by the end each character has undergone a substantial change. In terms of our model of 'order → chaos → reorder', the chaos might be slightly more subtle than in other genres as it is a reflective internal chaos, but the reordering is just as potent. At the end of Turgenev's *A Month in the Country*, Natalya is left alone, abandoned through her own actions. Those who are important to her have left the estate to continue with a new episode of their lives. Like *A Month in the County*, in Chekhov's plays, there is a sense of political change affecting the characters, in addition to the personal change that they are experiencing. The personal journey of the characters somehow relates to the political developments in Russia at the beginning of the twentieth century. In *The Cherry Orchard*,[13] for example, Lopakhin's buying of the cherry orchard is both a personal victory – the son of a serf becomes the owner of the estate he grew up on – and a symbol for a new Russia: the land will be used for the enjoyment of the middle classes, rather than as a fruitless farm for a now bankrupt family of the Russian land-owning gentry. The reordering is one of status, wealth and power on a private and public level. In both *A Month in the Country* and *The Cherry Orchard*, the person who has the most status has lost it all by the end of the play, reflecting the socio-economic changes happening in the country. Natalya has lost the men who award her power, and Ranevskaya has lost her family's heritage. This still fits within the framework of a comedy as by the end of the play Natalya has received her just rewards and Ranevskaya is happy – relieved to be free of responsibility. This subtle peripety represents a private reordering which is reflected in the more dramatic changes happening nationally at the time with the decline of Russia's aristocracy and the redistribution of wealth.

While the event which changes everything must be significant to have a lasting impact, it must also adhere to the rules of causality. Often in plays and films the pivotal event seems contrived, and the trust of the audience and the integrity of the story can be lost. Lopakhin buying the cherry orchard, the death of Konstatin in *The Seagull* and Vanya firing at the professor in *Uncle Vanya* are all incidents that come out of the narrative organically. We believe these choices that have been made. There is enough suggestion, build-up and anticipation to have the audience believe that these events have unfolded because of the characters' desires and subsequent actions rather than it being the hand of the writer manipulating the action in order to increase the drama. Often, there is so much micro-narrative and so many supplementary events in Chekhov's narrative that there is every chance that the audience will have lost the focus of the foreshadowing detail, so introducing this essential information early in the narrative will have a surprisingly subtle effect – the necessary detail has been supplied, but the audience have temporarily lost focus of it. For example, the significance of Lopakhin buying the cherry orchard is not immediate, until we remember a story that he told at the very beginning of the play, in which he spoke of his childlike reverence for Ranevskaya when she responded so kindly to an injury when he was disciplined by his father.

Exercise

Consider a plot-outline in which the characters' status and socio-economic power shift during the course of the narrative. The person with the most gravitas becomes the person with the least by the time the story finishes. What is it that precipitates this change? How do the characters feel about this complex shift in status? How can you embed the event which changes the *status quo* in the narrative without it appearing to be a *deus ex machina*?

One of the reasons that these stories are so effective is because the characters are portrayed with such depth. In *Aspects of the Novel*,[14] E. M. Forster explains the difference between 'flat characters' and 'round characters'. Even though Forster is writing about novels, it is worth bearing in mind that the world that Forster inhabited and the stories he was writing were not so dissimilar from some of the elements in Chekhov's stories: a diverse range of characters converging at a specific place during a specific time, and an examination of the everyday nuance in a world that is changing. In many ways, Chekhov and Forster might be seen as part of the same Modernist movement – examining the fabric of their changing world by exploring new forms. Forster suggests that 'flat characters' are more suitable for comedy, but that 'round characters' are something that can be created by having greater depth and doing unexpected things. While a 'flat character' never surprises, a 'round character' may take us by surprise with something they do. However, the test is that the character is 'capable of surprising in a convincing way'. This is reminiscent in a way of what was discussed when examining comic characters and comic archetypes. Effective characterisation involves a surprise or a paradox. Ranevskaya in *The Cherry Orchard* is penniless, but still acts as if she had wealth. For example, we hear that she still tips generously in restaurants even though she can hardly afford to do so. Lopakhin is a wealthy man and this wealth appears secure, but he still has the attitudes and deference of a serf. These surprises or paradoxes must always be believable and lead to a greater understanding of the person involved. Like in a real relationship, the audience learns more about the person as the story progresses: layers and aspects are revealed that we do not immediately see when we first encounter the person in the play or the film.

Exercise

Consider the situation that you invented in the previous exercise. Examine one of the characters. Think about a believable but surprising characteristic of one of these people. Write a scene in which this side of their personality becomes clear. How will you reveal this surprising characteristic? How will you ensure that it remains credible? What effect does this detail give to the scene as a whole? How do our attitudes to the person change?

Chekhov does not limit himself to complex characters. We also have 'flat characters' in his plays. Chekhov was a doctor by profession, and it sometimes feels as if he is identifying symptoms in his characters, and asking the audience to provide the diagnosis. In *The Cherry Orchard*, Gayev seems to remember past billiard games. This indicates how unable he is to live in the present, and that his previous life of wealth and leisure does not serve him well in the new Russia. Also in *The Cherry Orchard*, Varya – the adopted daughter of Ranevskaya – is always either on the verge of tears or sobbing. This is significant, as she is the only character to openly weep in all of Chekhov's plays. It is indicative, perhaps, of her lack of emotional and social stability. She seems disenfranchised, not belonging to any particular class. Brought up by the land-owning gentry, she is now engaged to Lopakhin who represents the new upwardly mobile middle classes, and she ends the play by taking a paid position as a housekeeper – something she has been doing for Ranevskaya out of a sense of duty for years anyway. The tears then are perhaps those of frustration as much as sadness – an inability to accept what is going to happen to her in the future, and to reconcile this with her past. When there are so many characters in a play, this technique of giving some of them recognisable characteristics seems sensible. The audience have an immediate shorthand way of keeping track of who is who. In many ways this is similar to Charles Dickens' way of keeping his numerous characters separate in the mind of the reader. For example, in *David Copperfield*,[15] Uriah Heep is known for his red hair and his catchphrase of 'ever so 'umble, sir, ever so 'umble'. As with Chekhov's characters, these recognisable features become telltale signs of inner qualities; in this case they reveal Uriah's insincerity and obsequiousness.

In Laura Wade's play *Posh*,[16] about members of the infamous Bullingdon Club, she successfully has twelve young men converge on the occasion of the dining club meeting. The audience follow the story that each of the men bring with ease. This is an indication of the skill with which Laura Wade writes these characters. Each has a characteristic or a story which is memorable, yet each is believable and the writing is subtle and nuanced.

Exercise

Still working with the same scene as in the previous exercise, consider a couple of characters and give them traits that reveal a deeper psychological state. Remember to keep this credible, even if the traits are quite quirky. Remember to repeat the character traits a couple of times. What is the effect of this on the scene? How does it change the tone of the writing?

Chekhov is skilled at writing about the ordinary. This is both a source of his comedy and his drama. While it appears that nothing happens for long periods in his plays, we see the interaction of every day being played out before us. Sometimes recognising this is enough to amuse us, interest us or make us laugh. There is an abundance of micro-narrative and supplementary events. It may appear uneconomic at first. However, everything has its significance in Chekhov. Even if a detail does not add to the constituent events, it will add something to the characters or the themes. It is also an important part of the 'lyric impulse'. This is when we see something that we have experienced ourselves in the story we are watching: loss, aspiration, unspoken desire, separation, envy. These are the emotions that we share. Regardless of the period in which the stories are set, these feelings are part of the collective experience of being human. We have all felt like Vanya (from *Uncle Vanya*) when he sees Astrov kissing Yelena, or felt like Sonya when she realizes that Astrov will never love her. Perhaps many of us have the aspiration of Lopakhin from *The Cherry Orchard* as we watch him realize that he can overturn the status quo and become the owner of the estate. There might be times when we feel as helpless and redundant as Ranevskaya, Gayev or Varya. Even if this experience is unspoken, the content of the dialogue conceals an underlying truth – something deeper which concerns not only what people say to one another, but also how they relate. There is much truth and drama in this seeming banality. A film by Woody Allen has a similar impact. Many micro-narratives are layered to explore the emotional states that we all recognize. On second or third viewing we realize the economy with which Woody Allen writes. Like Chekhov no detail is wasted, and every nuance reveals more depth about the people involved and the story that is unfolding.

Exercise

Consider an experience that might constitute a 'lyric impulse' – something that we have all experienced: for example, loss, separation, fear of abandonment, realising that we are in love, or realising that we are no longer in love. Write a scene that explores this impulse. There is no need to drive the overall narrative forward with the scene. Simply allow the scene to explore the confusion that this state of mind brings. The purpose of the scene is to give the audience a moment of recognition.

Exercise

Consider a bold emotional transaction that your characters might be experiencing. This might be something that occurred in the previous exercise. Write out the dialogue for this scene. Then rewrite this dialogue so that it has the same emotional transaction but this time have the characters talk about something completely different, so that the events of the scene are still clear, but hidden in the subtext.

The comedy that arises from these subtle situations is something that not everyone can relate to. Like the films of Woody Allen, Noah Baumbach or Wes Anderson, the comedy of Chekhov sits in unfulfilled hope. For example, in Woody Allen's *Hannah and Her Sisters*[17] there is much that is touching and funny about Elliot's futile courtship of Lee. Both are already married, and Lee remains oblivious of Elliot's real intention as he is buying her books and discussing poetry:

Elliot: For all my education, accomplishments and so-called wisdom, I can't fathom my own heart.

The pomposity and potential hubris of this line is what makes it so effective. The incongruous juxtaposition of Elliot's intellectual achievement and his emotional ignorance is both funny and true. Let us look at *Uncle Vanya* for comparable humour. Here is a moment in which Sonya explains her love for Astrov to Yelena:

Sonya: He comes every day, but he doesn't look at me. He doesn't see me. It's such torture! I've no hope – none, none at all! I've no strength left. I prayed all night. Often I go up to him and start the conversation myself. I look him straight in the face. I haven't the pride. I haven't the strength to control myself. Yesterday I couldn't stop myself confessing to Uncle Vanya. And all the servants know I'm in love with him. Everyone knows.
Yelena: What about him?
Sonya: No. He never notices me.[18]

The humour arises from two impulses. The first is the grand nature of the expression. It is almost bombastic or histrionic in the size of the drama expressed. This is then reduced to nothing with the statement that Astrov never notices Sonya. The second impulse concerns the gap between reality and fantasy. Both Elliot in *Hannah and Her Sisters* and Sonya in *Uncle Vanya* yearn for something that is not possible. It is not possible for Elliot because he will not leave Hannah, and it is not possible for Sonya because Astrov does not see her as a desirable woman. The permanence of this gap between reality and fantasy is potentially a source of sadness, but the persistence of the yearning is what gives rise to the comedy. There are less subtle examples which illustrate this comic impulse more clearly. In *Twelfth Night*, Malvolio becomes convinced that Olivia loves him, even though the union between them is preposterous. In *Gavin and Stacey*,[19] Nessa and Smithy have had a child and clearly care for each other, but they convince themselves that they are not compatible. Their relationship is in many ways more moving and real than the relationship between Gavin and Stacey.

In *The Office*, David Brent believes himself to be a significant figure in British comedy, even though he is simply a manager in a suburban stationery warehouse. The gap between reality and fantasy is a source of comedy in which disappointment is inevitable. This disappointment is somehow funny. It is the comedy equivalent of the hubris that we find in tragedy. The fall from grace does not result in death but instead in wounded pride and disappointment. It would seem that this is an archetypal experience – the sad clown at the circus is perhaps one of the first examples that we encounter. We laugh at our own folly, and we are relieved that this time it is not us. Lena Dunham has reinvented this comic impulse for a new generation. The television comedy, *Girls*,[20] is an antidote to the glossy US television sitcoms. The four young women seem to remain relatively cheerful as they move from one disappointment to another.

Exercise

Write a monologue for one of your characters. Let them explain to another character an aspiration or a hope. Make sure that achieving this aspiration is in no way possible, despite the belief of the character. Elaborate on the detail, and be specific. At what point does this begin to be funny?

It is perhaps worth mentioning that Chekhov saw his plays as comedies also because of the changing situation in Russia. The dramaturgical significance of the plays' endings served the political upheaval of the time. Chekhov came from the social class that was growing in wealth and status following the Emancipation Reform of 1861. He was a descendant of the serf class, and so for him seeing this class become educated, or earn wealth and buy land was a cause of celebration. So Vanya's victory on Sonya's behalf, or Lopakhin's purchase of the cherry orchard is seen as a positive occurrence in the changing landscape of Russia. For Chekhov the distribution of wealth is flowing in the preferred direction. The opposite is true of Stanislavsky, who first directed these plays. For him, the content of these stories was deeply upsetting, as this was his social class that was becoming less wealthy and politically less relevant.

Let us briefly return to the economy of writing in Chekhov. The use of micro-narrative and supplementary events build to provide us with a detailed picture of a complex world. No element is wasted, and every character's story reaches a conclusion which reveals the transformation that has happened as a result of the choices and events in the play. This principle of economy is known as Chekhov's gun:

> To make a face out of marble means to remove from that piece of marble everything that is not a face. Remove everything that has no relevance to the story. If you say in the first chapter that there is a rifle hanging on the wall, in the second or third chapter it absolutely must go off. If it's not going to be fired, it shouldn't be hanging there.[21]

This economy might be desired by all writers regardless of the genre that is being engaged with. The economy increases the effect of the all-important causality. The narrative keeps an inherent integrity, as less can be seen as inventions by the writer in order to keep the plot progressing. All plot elements assist the organic progression of the plot.

This is not to imply that Chekhov's writing lacks theatricality or does not employ narrative devices. Chekhov's narrative is crafted with agility and skill. I have included a comparison showing the similarities between Chekhov and Shakespeare. The table at the end of this chapter juxtaposes these narrative techniques. A comparison serves to show how much well-crafted stories have in common regardless of the differences in culture and period. An effective and engaging story for the Elizabethans has much in common with that for an early-twentieth-century Russian audience. These are the narrative devices that remain essential for dramatists.

Exercise

Consider the list of narrative devices below. Choose one of these techniques and rewrite one of your scenes from this chapter, but including this device. How does it improve the efficacy of the scene? What is the benefit for the audience?

Checklist

Here is a checklist for building a story in a way that reflects some Chekhovian techniques and concerns:

- A variety of characters converge on a specific place where they are in some way isolated or stranded.
- Out of the boredom various events arise – some of these are supplementary events and some are constituent events.
- Some of the characters contain a surprising, but believable, paradox. Others have a particular trait that reveals something about their psychological state.
- By the end of the story, there has been a socio-economic reordering. The power is distributed differently at the end.
- The meaning of dialogue is often contained in the subtext, rather than overtly spoken.
- Various narrative techniques are employed to develop the various strands of the story.
- Each character's development is clear. Most have changed in some way by the end.
- Past events affect the present, and unresolved issues from many years ago find a sense of resolve.

Narrative Techiques in Shakespeare and Chekhov

Please note: this is not a definitive list, and not all Shakespeare's plays that involve each narrative technique have been listed.

	Shakespeare	Chekhov
1. The arrival of characters as a point of entry and/or a catalyst for change.	*Much Ado About Nothing* *The Tempest* *Twelfth Night*	*The Cherry Orchard* *Uncle Vanya* *The Seagull*
2. Spectacle is used as a narrative hook.	*The Tempest* *Romeo and Juliet* *Hamlet*	
3. Narrative exposition in the form of a speech/monologue	*The Tempest*	*The Cherry Orchard* *The Seagull*
4. A new order is established by the end of the play.	Political: *Hamlet, Henry IV part 2, Richard II,* *Richard III* Personal: *Twelfth Night, Much Ado about Nothing*	Personal: *Three Sisters* *Uncle Vanya* Financial: *The Cherry Orchard*
5. Point of view of different social classes is represented.	*The Tempest* *Romeo and Juliet*	*The Cherry Orchard* *The Seagull*

(Continued)

	Shakespeare	Chekhov
6. The convergence of the otherwise incompatible.	*Much Ado About Nothing* *Henry IV parts 1 and 2*	*The Cherry Orchard*
7. Narrative with multiple strands.	*The Tempest* *Cymbeline*	*Uncle Vanya* *The Seagull*
8. Spectacle.	Masque sequences: *The Tempest* *The Winter's Tale* *The Two Noble Kinsmen*	*The Cherry Orchard* (the party scene)
9. Meta-textuality.	*A Midsummer Night's Dream* *Hamlet*	*The Seagull*
10. Frequent tonal change.	*King Lear* *Romeo and Juliet*	*The Cherry Orchard* *Uncle Vanya*
11. Onstage violence.	*Romeo and Juliet* *Titus Andronicus*	*Uncle Vanya* *The Seagull*

11

ARRIVALS AND DEPARTURES: THE CHIVALRIC ROMANCE AND THE PASTORAL

Discussing these two distinct genres in the same chapter might seem to be an odd decision, but they represent two different sides of the same coin. Both involve a departure from home and then a return of sorts. With the Pastoral the characters literally return to where they started from and in the Chivalric Romance, the hero or heroine in some way returns to the circumstances of their birth, and, by doing so, there is a figurative homecoming. This narrative trope of returning home is a powerful one. Whether it is the return of Odysseus in Homer's epic or the imminent return of Prospero in *The Tempest*, the homecoming marks a moment of reconciliation or reunion – a reordering that resolves the chaos of being in transit or homeless. The emotional power of telling a story of a return is great. It resonates with the audience as a something everyone has experience of, and exploits one of our most profound fears – being without a home.

The form of the Chivalric Romance is something that is known to us as one of our most familiar stories. The hero leaves home and after an adventure involving some sort of test, learns an important truth about themselves or their family. Examples fitting this pattern are wide-raging and diverse: Homeric narrative, German and French medieval epics, Shakespeare's *Two Noble Kinsmen* or *All's Well that Ends Well*, *The Wizard of Oz*,[1] *The Lord of the Rings*,[2] *Indiana Jones*,[3] *Star Wars: Episonde IV – A New Hope*,[4] or *Harry Potter*.[5] For some, this is the archetypal story which forms the basis of all narrative: Joseph Campbell,[6] Christopher Vogler,[7] John Yorke.[8] These theorists make a convincing argument for the quest story being the archetypal story, but we are engaging with an even simpler form for story than that of the quest narrative:

a structure of order → chaos → reorder

Which is driven by people making choices. Also my interpretation of how these stories are structured differs slightly in that I do not concentrate on some of the stages of the hero's journey that the others identify as an important part of the story.

While discussing the Chivalric Romance, we will focus on *Star Wars* and *The Wizard of Oz*. There will also be some reference to *Parzival*[9] – the medieval German epic by Wolfram von Eschenbach, and *Tristan*[10] by Gottfried von Strassburg. Whether you are aware of these German stories through Wagner's adaptations, or whether you are completely unfamiliar with these German stories, I would urge you to read them in a modern translation. For anyone interested in how story functions, the rewards of reading these German epics are plenty. They also show how the template was already in place for current popular epics such as *The Lord of the Rings*, *Harry Potter* and the *Twilight Saga*. If *Parzival* seems too daunting, I would suggest beginning with Gottfried von Strassburg's *Tristan* – a much more accessible story of a quest involving a love which is doomed from the beginning.

The chivalric code is at the heart of these stories, even if this is covertly the case. The chivalric code embodies the idea that as a result of a quest, the hero will ultimately become a better person. The notion of love is also at the centre of the chivalric code in that it is something that improves the moral worth of the couple. The knight would fall in love with someone who is unobtainable in terms of status, so he would need to prove himself to be worthy of the prize he was bidding for. Successfully completing the quest would be proof that he has become more virtuous. According to medieval Catholicism, God is present in any relationship, and a committed and fulfilling relationship is seen as an act of worship. It is interesting, then, with the proof of love and virtue being so important with God so present, that infidelity should be such a feature of these stories: *Gawain and the Green Knight*,[11] the Arthurian legends and *Tristan* all involve the temptation to commit infidelity – a temptation which is often succumbed to. Perhaps as moral improvement on the hero's journey is an archetypal story, so is the hero's fall.

Exercise

Imagine a modern-day context which tests the honour of a protagonist. Without getting too involved in exposition, write a scene in which a character must make a choice, and this choice is indicative of the character's morality. How do moral values change by making this choice? Does this make the protagonist less or more sympathetic to an audience? Does a situation involving a moral choice automatically make for a dramatic situation?

The initial stage of the Chivalric Romance is that of comfortable routine. Our protagonist seems to have their path already set, as they are comfortable in their daily life. Despite this relative stability, there is something amiss in their lives. In *The Wizard of Oz*, Dorothy is restless and lonely living on her aunt's farm; in *Star Wars*, Luke Skywalker is also restless, but comfortable helping his uncle, unaware of his father's history as a Jedi. It is interesting to note that in these iconic films, the routine that both protagonists are involved in is based on a farm. In both these examples, the protagonists are in some way outsiders, not really fitting in to their own environment, and the farm is the starting place for the adventure. Something then happens which breaks them out of their routine. For Dorothy it is Miss Gulch taking her dog, Toto, and then the arrival of the tornado. For Luke it is buying the C3PO droid, and then finding the message for Obi-Wan Kenobi from Princess Leia. In terms of causality, these initial opening events do not fit in with our ideal pattern. We have discussed the need for causality in stories – that one event is the logical consequence of a character's decision, and that this then leads to a narrative with integrity which satisfies its audience. The tornado and the chance buying of a droid are events which occur randomly. The mechanics of the narrative depends, then, on how the characters react to a coincidental intervention. The coincidental nature of this initial event is made clear in *Star Wars*. Luke's uncle initially chooses another droid which promptly explodes before they can take it away. Had this droid never exploded, the message from Leia would never have been found, and Luke would have perished in the raid on his farm like his uncle and his aunt. Perhaps this is a reminder that coincidence is a part of life, and the stories we inhabit are full of chance. A hero is made because of how he or she reacts when opportunity or challenge arises – it is the choices that constitute a story.

Exercise

Write a scene in which your protagonist is settled in his or her routine, but at the same time somewhat restless and dissatisfied. How are you able to balance these two paradoxical elements? It is the routine that keeps the character safe, but at the same time they do not value safety. Write an event which takes the main character out of this routine. If possible, make the event a result of the character's choice, rather than an extraneous incident which is clearly invented by you. This makes your story organic, and makes the main character responsible for the story immediately.

Through the event that interrupts the routine – or the *inciting incident* as some theorists refer to it – the hero is introduced to the teacher or guide who inducts them in the ways of the new world that they inhabit. This is someone who escorts the protagonist over the threshold and into adventure. For Dorothy, it is Glinda the fairy, and for Luke it is Obi-Wan Kenobi. Both serve to provide explanations and guidance, and reveal the first of the quests. This information is as much for the benefit of the audience as it is for the benefit of the character on the adventure. Dorothy learns that by killing the Witch of the East and inheriting her slippers, she will be pursued by the Wicked Witch of the West, and must go to the Wizard of Oz for help. Luke learns that his father was a Jedi, and that he must set out to rescue Princess Leia at the same time as beginning his Jedi training with Obi-Wan Kenobi. This initial quest is almost a folly, and its success or failure is almost immaterial.

Exercise

Following on from the previous exercise, who does your character meet who will act as a guide or a teacher? Write the scene in which your protagonist learns something significant now that they no longer have their routine to protect them. A matter must arise that demands their immediate attention.

The purpose of this initial quest is to reveal the details of the second quest. The second quest is the challenge which really matters. The protagonist will be tested to a degree that makes them face a primal fear, and in doing so, unlock some information about themselves. Dorothy finds the Wizard but then has to bring back the Witch's broom – a quest that seems perilously unfair for a young woman and is something that can only be done with courage, tenacity and trust in her companions. Luke has to destroy the Death Star. The first part of the adventure is then eclipsed in the audience's perception of the story as the second quest reveals itself to be the real challenge. It is almost as if the audience is being prepared to fully appreciate the story. The first test has been tough, but the second test will demand something beyond expectation from the protagonist as it is such a seemingly impossible task, and perhaps even unfair after the first task has been successfully completed.

It is the attempt that defines the second quest, and the courage which is required to overcome (sometimes literally) insurmountable odds. Whether the protagonist succeeds or not is almost incidental. This is the remarkable element of German Chivalric Romance – the protagonists fail repeatedly. In the initial phase of the story, Parzival's failures are almost comical. In fact, he nearly succeeds in the quest ahead of time, but for his failure to ask the key question of Anfortas, the Grail King. Tristan is successful in any task of chivalry, but is doomed to remain a failure in his own personal quest as he has fallen in love with the king's wife. The important factor is what has been learnt and how the protagonist has changed. By the end of the story, Parzival learns that he is part of the Grail lineage. Tristan ends his life unfulfilled by a relationship mirroring the circumstances of his conception. Dorothy learns that there is no place like home, and if it cannot be found in your own back yard there is no point looking for it in the first place. Luke learns what can be overcome when he trusts the Force. This transformation experienced by the protagonist is at the heart of the Chivalric Romance. He or she has changed dramatically by the end of the story: Dorothy is appreciative of the love and support of her family, and aware of what her tenacity might achieve; Luke's eyes have been opened to a greater universe and a more substantial struggle than he was previously aware of. This fits with our two essential patterns of narrative:

$$order \rightarrow chaos \rightarrow reorder$$

and

$$choice \rightarrow consequence \rightarrow change$$

In a Chivalric Romance, the outer world is not necessarily that which is reordered. The universe might be a safer place with the destruction of the Death Star, but the Empire continues to exert its tyranny. The reordering has happened within Luke Skywalker, and the Rebel Alliance has gained a new hero. If the reordering happens within the character of the protagonist, so does the chaos. Leaving home, fulfilling the quest and completing the task are representative of the chaos which then results in the development and growth of the reordering. Something has to break down in order for there to be a breakthrough. The quest itself involves a series of choices which lead to different potential consequences. The initial choice of course is the decision to accept the challenge. Had Dorothy not gone looking for Toto, she would not have been vulnerable to the tornado; had Luke not gone looking for Obi-Wan Kenobi, he would have perished in the raid on the farm. It is this initial choice which shows first the hero's resolve, resourcefulness and tenacity – qualities that will be tested repeatedly on the quest.

Exercise

Once the initial problem is resolved, what is the real challenge that your protagonist will face? This problem or test must be as demanding as you can possibly imagine for the character. Their tenacity and resolve must be tested, and they must face a pathological fear or character trait. Do they succeed or fail? What have they learnt about themselves, or their heritage?

Before we leave the Chivalric Romance, it is worth mentioning how the quest often focuses on one 'magic' object: ruby slippers, a magic ring, a goblet of fire, the Holy Grail, a magic potion. Often the protagonist is under the misapprehension that the object will bring the solution. However, it is the journey itself which results in the transformation.

The table below is intended to put the stages of the Chivalric Romance into focus.

	Tristan	Star Wars – A New Hope	The Wizard of Oz
The hero is apparently innocent in his/her set routine.	Tristan in Parmenie	Luke on Tatooine – living with his uncle and aunt	Dorothy with the farmhands on the farm in Kansas
An unexpected event takes them out of this routine.	Tristan is kidnapped by pirates.	The buying of the R2D2 and C3P0 droids.	Miss Gulch taking Toto

(Continued)

	Tristan	Star Wars – A New Hope	The Wizard of Oz
A teacher or guardian takes them over the threshold and into a new world.	The Marshal Rual (and also perhaps King Mark)	Obi-Wan 'Ben' Kenobi	Glinda
The beginning of the quest.	To go to Ireland to fetch Isolde for King Mark	Going to rescue Princess Leia	Going to find the Wizard of Oz
The real quest is revealed.	To live with the woman he loves All other quests are a distraction.	Destroying the Death Star	Bringing back the witch's broom
The success or failure of the quest is eclipsed by the knowledge that the quest brings.	It is his family's destiny that he will be a tragic lover. He dies as he was conceived.	That he will carry the values of the Jedi into the fight against the Empire	That there is no place like home

Like the Chivalric Romance coming out of Homeric narrative, the Pastoral also comes to us from classical origins. Theocritus' poems depict the lives of Sicilian shepherds and Virgil's *Eclogues* establish the convention of the Pastoral:

> an elaborately conventional poem expressing an urban poet's nostalgic image of the peace and tranquillity of the life of shepherds and other rural folk in an idealised natural setting.[12]

The classical 'Golden Age' is mixed with Christian allegory: return to the Garden of Eden; a sense of the innocence of the rural meeting the possible corruption of the court; redemption; and Christ as the Good Shepherd. We encounter the form in the Renaissance with Spenser's *The Shepherd's Calendar* (1579) and Sir Philip Sidney's *Arcadia* (1581–4). Shakespeare adheres to the conventions of the Pastoral in *As you Like it*, *A Midsummer Night's Dream*, *The Winter's Tale* and *Cymbeline. The Tempest* may also arguably also be viewed as a Pastoral.

The Pastoral has much in common with the Chivalric Romance, but it may also mix in elements from Romantic Comedy. Both the Pastoral and the Chivalric Romance begin with a journey. In the Pastoral, the protagonist comes from a courtly (or urban) environment and ventures into a rural landscape. The teacher in this case is usually a kindly elderly shepherd who is teaching covertly through his wisdom and humility, rather than being a deliberate guide. Through exposure to the simpler, more holistic way of living, the protagonist changes for the better, and will return to the city with a new and more healthy perspective. Within our contemporary storytelling, the Pastoral is nearly as ubiquitous as the Chivalric Romance: for example, most Pixar films (*Cars*,[13] *Finding Nemo*,[14] *WALL-E*,[15] *Monster's Inc.*[16]) fit into this genre. The reason why these are considered Pastorals rather than Chivalric Romances is because of the way the journey begins, and the level of integration with the newly discovered world. Nemo is captured rather than sent on a quest, and he integrates into the new community in the dentist's fish tank. Marlon goes looking for him and meets along the way several characters who challenge his 'urban' world view, most notably the turtles, who teach him how to literally and figuratively 'go with the flow'. *WALL-E* is a clever subversion of the Pastoral with WALL-E taking a little piece of nature up to the space station, and bringing the whole of humanity back to a more natural and organic life, as they learn to leave their screens and come and engage once again with the earth. There is no double quest, no guide to escort the protagonist over the threshold and no magic object. However there is still a sense of the protagonist learning and changing for the better, having been exposed to a more natural and innocent way of living.

In Shakespeare's *As You Like It*, Rosalind is banished from court by her uncle. Her cousin Celia accompanies her into the forest of Arden where Rosalind's father and the remaining exiled court are now living. Duke Senior explains the relief he feels living this rural life:

> And this our life exempt from public haunt
> Finds tongues in trees, books in the running brooks,
> Sermons in stones and good in every thing.
> I would not change it.[17]

This is a familiar trope in the Pastoral; the complex needs of courtly life are sufficiently replaced by the elements of the countryside. Gonzalo makes a similar speech in *The Tempest*. Celia has fallen in love with Orlando who has also fled the court, and disguised as a boy, she teaches him how to woo so that she might cure him of his love for her. This element of transgender disguise and wooing is a traditional element of this genre. In Sir Philip Sidney's *Arcadia*, Duke Basilus of Arcadia has hidden himself in the forest in order to escape the Oracle's prediction of his downfall. His daughters are then courted by their two noble cousins, Pyrocles and Musidorus, who disguise themselves in order to get close to them. In *As You Like It*, the court is transformed by a sojourn in the countryside. Reconciliation, romance and reunion are the result. Duke Senior is reconciled with his reformed despotic brother. Rosalind and Celia take their first steps into responsible adulthood as they both return to court to be married. There is a sense of hope that the countryside has transformed them all into better people, and their lives at court will be less expedient and more wholesome. The exception to this in Shakespeare's Pastorals is to be found in *The Tempest*. Through the reconciliation of Prospero with his brother we might imagine that Milan will be a better place, but Miranda seems to have lost her innocence through her encounter with Ferdinand, and learnt the expedient ways of the court. At the end of the play, they are revealed playing chess, and Miranda accuses Ferdinand of cheating. He denies this. Miranda replies:

> Yes, for a score of kingdoms you should wrangle,
> And I would call it fair play.[18]

Miranda is now willing to accept Ferdinand's political manoeuvring as something essential to courtly life. She concedes that her loyalty to him is such that she will lie for him and not acknowledge the objective truth.

Hart of Dixie[19] is a highly successful American television series. Rachel Bilson plays Dr Zoe Hart, a surgeon from New York whose dynamic career stalls, and so she accepts a job as a general practitioner in town of Bluebell, Alabama. Every episode trades on Zoe's sophisticated city attitude clashing with the old-fashioned rural traditions. Her integration within the community is slow and painful, and any attempts result in disaster. Mixed in with the Pastoral is also an element of Comedy of Manners and Romantic Comedy: Zoe falls in love with George, the local town lawyer who is resisting his father's wishes that he practice in a more urban legal practice. George is engaged to Lemon, an ambitious young member of the local community whose ways are gently satirized. Meanwhile, Wade a local Lothario, has fallen haplessly in love with Zoe. The mayor of the town is a former basketball player who has a pet crocodile. The morality of the series corresponds exactly to that of the traditional Pastoral. The quirks and customs of the people local to Bluebell are portrayed as eccentric, or even mildly ridiculous, but there is no doubt that living in such a close community is more healthy, and ultimately more edifying, than life in the city. Infidelity is always a temptation, but there is a hopeful sense that in this rural idyll, the best aspects in each character will triumph. At the end of the first season, Zoe confronts the man she considers her father – a high-powered surgeon. He expresses his disappointment that her career is not developing as he might have wished, but he also expresses his appreciation of the young woman that Zoe is turning into.

The relationship with our fundamental pattern of order → chaos → reorder is clear. The flight into the countryside represents an internal and external chaos which is then reordered when the character returns to the city or court. In terms of this structure, the rural environment represents a liminal space in which the protagonist can prepare to cross a threshold. By entering this rural world, and experiencing the disorientation that accompanies the strangeness of it, the protagonist almost regresses to a child-like state from which they can grow and a new phase of their life can begin.

Checklist

Here are two checklists for you to consider if you are writing according to the principles of the Chivalric Romance or the Pastoral.

The Chivalric Romance

- The protagonist is supported by a clear routine or way of life. They have a feeling that they do not really fit in, and are different from those around them.
- An event breaks them out of the routine and the quest begins.
- They meet a teacher or guide who introduces them to a new world.
- The first quest of challenge begins.
- This leads to the second quest which is more substantial.
- Regardless of success or failure, the protagonist learns something significant about themselves or their family.

The Pastoral

- The protagonist is secure and happy in their urban environment. They inhabit a particularly insular world.
- An event causes them to flee into the countryside.
- A new world is discovered which is simpler and more wholesome than the world the protagonist is accustomed to.
- There may be some elements of disguise and/or romance.
- The protagonist returns to the urban environment to begin a new phase of their life, having benefited from what they have learnt.

A FINAL THOUGHT

There are many different ways to peel and dice a pineapple. This book represents only one of many ways to engage dramaturgically with story. However, in all the years that I have been teaching and working in script development, two questions have never failed to sharpen a writer's approach to what they are writing:

- How are the stages of order, chaos and reorder shaped in this story?
- Where do your characters have to make choices?

These two questions will pull any slight blurry script into focus.

My hope is that you are thinking about story structure differently, and new shapes are forming in your mind when you write, or when you go to the theatre or the cinema. I hope that you now have these shapes and structures to rely on, and that you will continue to consider the magic of genre.

APPENDIX 1
MISCELLANEOUS GENRES
AND HYBRIDS

Expressionism

This is a hybrid of the Chivalric Romance and Tragedy, but with a significant tonal variation. It occurred because artists wanted an alternative to realism. The protagonist has a routine which is almost mechanical. This is then interrupted and the character goes on a journey which results in a degree of success and self-knowledge, but also death. The other characters are named by their relationship with the protagonist, rather than given names. This puts the protagonist firmly at the centre of their universe, as the story is told from their point of view. Expressionism is a reaction to industrialisation – human beings are viewed as anonymous and expendable and there is a need to break free from the system that simultaneously supports and imprisons them. However, breaking free results in death. The lines are short (telegrammatic), and characters rarely give speeches. The classic Vampire film, *Nosferatu*,[1] is Expressionist. Georg Kaiser is perhaps the most well-known German expressionist playwright. Brecht's Epic Theatre is a development of Expressionism. It adds self-conscious theatrical devices and arguments presented as dialectics. Perhaps the best way of understanding this development is watching the television series, *The Simpsons*,[2] which actually adheres to most elements of the Expressionist template.

The Horror Film

This is the contemporary version of the Jacobean Tragedy. The monster is a mysterious but distinct figure, and like Jacobean Tragedy, the virtue of young women is embedded in the narrative. The most 'virtuous' in terms of her sexuality is the one who survives; the most experienced and least 'virtuous' is most likely to be the one who is killed first. The patterns and tropes of horror films make it one of the most formulaic of all contemporary film genres. This gives rise to films such as *The Cabin in the Woods*[3] and the *Scream*[4] franchise which deconstruct and subvert with meta-textual references.

Absurdism

Theatre of the Absurd is the only genre which does not adhere to the structure of order → chaos → reorder. The sense of confusion following the First World War meant the notion of a reordering became somewhat redundant. This leaves us with a short period of drama which explores existential themes – the idea that we might be cosmically abandoned and that there is no order in the universe.

Hyper-Realism

This is a late-twentieth-century genre which is a further development of Expressionism. The most obvious exponent of this is Bernard-Maire Koltes. His play *Roberto Zucco*[5] sets the template for many writers to follow, for example, Sarah Kane and Mark Ravenhill. Many of Pinter's plays can be seen as Hyper-realist. These stories involve a protagonist whose routine is interrupted and their ordered life turns into chaos. Often the reordering is only resolved with death. Like Expressionism, the lines are short (telegrammatic). The stories always involve extreme acts of violence, and the content is often sexually explicit.

The Gangster Film or Drama of Succession

Whether it is Shakespeare's History plays, *The Sopranos* or *The Godfather,* this genre is a close relative of the Revenge Tragedy, but its main concern is who succeeds to the throne, or who becomes head of the mafia family. The story begins with the current ruler doing something which initiates an overthrow. The narrative is then involved with the success or failure of this overthrow, and the implications of the new succession. Shakespeare's *Richard II* begins with the exile of Bolingbroke and Mowbray. It ends with Bolingbroke becoming Henry IV. The structure of order → chaos → reorder is clearly embedded in the narrative.

The Thriller

The thriller maintains suspense by keeping the audience asking 'how did it happen', as much as 'what will happen next'. The narrative begins in chaos. Someone has been murdered, and we must discover who has been the perpetrator and why. Our point of view is that of the detective. The conclusion often involves a *deus ex machina*, as an essential piece of information has been withheld so that the least likely suspect remains a surprise.

The locked-room whodunnit is a traditional variation on this genre. In order to limit the number of suspects, the murder occurs in a locked room. The detective must eliminate suspicion from each of the suspects before a twist in the plot reveals who the murderer is. *The Girl with the Dragon Tattoo* fits into this traditional structure. There have been some more sophisticated variations of this genre on television. The amount of time needed for a whole series suits the complexity of the story, as exemplified in *The Killing, The Bridge, Broadchurch* and *The Fall*. Chaos is reordered once justice has been restored, and the murderer caught and punished. In the first series of *The Killing* and *The Fall*, there was no resolve. In the case of *The Killing*, this led to an audience outcry, and production of the second series was brought forward. Regardless of the complexities of the thriller, there is usually a sense of disappointment towards the end, as the final essential piece of information is revealed, and many of the plot strands are seen as 'red herrings'. Occasionally, this genre turns into a Revenge Tragedy as the story progresses. Revealing the examples in which this is the case would spoil the story.

The Rites of Passage Story

The idea of individuation is present in most stories in some way. It is a key element to the Chivalric Romance and the Pastoral. The protagonist returns from the adventure older and wiser than when they set out. Shakespeare's first part of *Henry IV* is both a History play (Succession Drama) and a rites of passage story. The protagonist in the rites of passage story does not necessarily go on an adventure; we simply see them making choices, experience things for the first time, and changing. Although they were not writing for performance, the novels of Dickens and Austin might all be considered to fit into this genre, which may account for their frequent dramatisation. There have been many successful examples of this on US television, such as *Dawson's Creek*,[6] *90210*[7] and *The OC*.[8] The new order which occurs is a loss of some of the elements of childhood or youth and assuming some of the responsibilities of adulthood.

The Superhero Story

The superhero genre is a mix of Chivalric Romance and Revenge Tragedy. It is essential to remember that the superhero and the supervillain are in some way responsible for each other's creation.

APPENDIX 2
OTHER THEORIES AND OTHER APPROACHES

Joseph Campbell, *The Hero with a Thousand Faces*[1]

George Lucas credits Campbell as his inspiration when writing the first of the *Star Wars* movies. Campbell explains that there is one archetypal myth which all human cultures seem to share. This is the 'hero's journey'. Campbell uses the ideas of Carl G. Jung to illuminate the monomyth, and breaks the stages of the stories down in a similar way to those that are described in the chapter on Chivalric Romance. Campbell's concern is not screenwriting or playwriting, and this is a dense and difficult collection of writings if you are not used to engaging with Jungian terminology. His theories primarily engage with the importance of storytelling and myth.

Syd Field, *Screenplay: The Foundations of Screenwriting*[2]

Field is an exponent of the three-act structure. He advises that a screenplay has a set-up, a confrontation and a resolution, with two significant plot points occurring at the end of first and second acts. The second of these plot points will cause a turnaround (or periperty) for the protagonist, leading them into crisis. The examples are numerous, and come from contemporary and classic films. It is a clear and convincing read, but much more prescriptive than the structures presented in *Genre*.

Robert McKee, *Story*[3]

McKee is known for his 'story seminar'; a three-day seminar on screenwriting which he has delivered all over the world in the past twenty-five years. The book reads like a transcribed lecture, and I imagine that it is compelling when delivered in one of McKee's 'performances'. It engages with the 'classical design' of story structure, or what Mckee refers to as 'Archplot'. He borrows the phrase 'inciting incident' from John Howard Lawson, and presents a prescriptive structure which McKee argues is true for all effective writing.

Christopher Vogler, *The Writer's Journey*[4]

Vogler makes the writings of Jung and Joseph Campbell accessible to writers and storytellers. The story is broken down into five acts, beginning with the hero's call to adventure, and concluding with his or her return. The various stages of the plot are described as 'thresholds'.

Blake Snyder, *Save the Cat!*[5]

This is a highly prescriptive guide to screenwriting. The title refers to having the protagonist 'save the cat' in the first act in order to create immediate empathy with the audience. There is a very brief discussion of ten genres, and some notes on archetypal characters. However, the value of this book is in its tone: it is informal, anecdotal and chatty. It makes for a blunt and polemical read about story structure in film.

Christopher Booker, *The Seven Basic Plots: Why We Tell Stories*[6]

Booker explores the seven 'basic stories'. This is a similar idea to that in *Genre*, but his distinctions seem limited more to film. The impulse is similar; making links between stories which have been written several hundred years apart. The analysis is detailed, and the examples are clear. The final part is a fascinating discussion of 'aberrant' stories – stories that have gone amiss and do not provide satisfactory endings.

John Yorke, *Into the Woods: A Five Act Journey into Story*[7]

Yorke uses the image of going into the woods in a way that is similar to our discussion of chaos in *Genre*. He develops the idea of the five-act structure, and focuses on peripety – or what has changed for the protagonist in each act. Yorke refers to this as the 'Roadmap of Change', and he suggests that the turnaround is always the same for each act. For example, act one involves the change from 'no knowledge' to 'awakening'; act two involves the change from 'doubt' to 'acceptance'.

Noël Greig, Playwriting *A Practical Guide*[8]

Grieg offers a step-by-step guide to writing a play. There are clear exercises accompanying each stage, and examples and outcomes are described. Themes, issues, character and story are all handled in this pragmatic way. There is also an invaluable section on redrafting.

David Edgar, *How Plays Work*[9]

Edgar discusses the 'common architecture' of storytelling, focusing on playwriting. He begins with the audience's expectations which make for a convincing argument of why structure is important: we assess a play according to its plausibility, coherence and conventionality. Edgar then proceeds to examine action, character and structure. There is an in-depth and practical chapter on genre.

H. Porter Abbott, *The Cambridge Introduction to Narrative*[10]

Even though this book is meant to sharpen analytical skills rather than be used as a 'how to' guide, it is recommended reading for all writers. Abbott explains with clarity and precision the principles of narrative. Looking at how stories are constructed regardless of whether they are novels, plays or films is illuminating. I suggest that this introduction to narrative might solve more issues with your script than some of the books that are dedicated to screenwriting or scriptwriting.

NOTES

Chapter 1

1. Field, Syd, *Screenplay, The Foundations of Screenwriting*, New York: Random House, 1979.
2. McKee, Robert, *Story*, London: Methuen, 1997.
3. Dworkin, Susan, *Making Tootsie*, New York: Newmarket Press, 2012.
4. Abbott, H. Porter, *The Cambridge Introduction to Narrative*, 2nd edn, Cambridge: Cambridge University Press, 2008.
5. *War of the Worlds*, dir. Byron Haskin, Paramount Pictures, 1953, or *War of the Worlds*, dir. Steven Spielberg, Paramount Pictures, Dreamworks SKG, Amblin Entertainment, 2005.
6. *Sleepless in Seattle*, dir. Nora Ephron, Tristar Pictures, 1993.
7. *Sabrina*, dir. Billy Wilder, Paramount Pictures, 1954.
8. *Star Wars: Episode IV – A New Hope*, dir. George Lucas, Lucas Film, Twentieth Century Fox, 1977.
9. Sophocles, *The Theban Plays* (trans. E. Watling), London: Penguin Classics, 1973.
10. Aeschylus, *The Oresteia* (trans. Robert Fagles), London: Penguin Classics, 1977.
11. *Frasier*, created by David Angell, Peter Casey and David Lee, Paramount, 1993–2004.
12. *Clueless*, dir. Amy Heckerling, Paramount Pictures, 1995.
13. *Mean Girls*, dir. Mark Waters, Paramount Pictures, M.G. Films, 2004.
14. Wycherley, William, *The Country Wife*, London: Methuen Drama, 2003.
15. Wilde, Oscar, *The Importance of Being Earnest*, London: Penguin, 1964.
16. *Tootsie*, dir. Sydney Pollack, Columbia Pictures Corporation and Mirage/Punch Production, 1982.
17. *90210* created by Jeff Judah, Gabe Sachs and Darren Star, Sachs/Judah Productions, CBS Productions. 2008–13.
18. *Saw*, dir. James Wan, Evolution Entertainment, Saw Productions, Twisted Pictures, 2005.
19. *Curb Your Enthusiasm*, created by Larry David, HBO films, 2000–.
20. Freire, Paulo, *The Pedagogy of the Oppressed*, London: Penguin, 1996.
21. *Friends*, created by David Crane and Marta Kauffman, Warner Bros Television, Bright/Kauffman/Crane Productions, 1994–2004.
22. *Bullet Boy*, dir. Saul Dibb, BBC Films, UK Film Council, 2004.
23. *Storm Damage*, dir. Simon Cellan Jones, BBC Films, 2000.
24. 'Some uncommon television images and the drench hypothesis' by Greenberg B.S. in Oskamp, S. (ed.), 'Applied social psychology annual: Television as a social issue (Vol 8)' Newbury Park, Sage Publications.
25. *Alien 3*, dir. David Fincher, Twentieth Century Fox, Brandywine Productions, 1992.
26. *The Bourne Legacy*, dir. Tony Gilroy, Universal Pictures, Relativity Media, 2012.
27. *Prometheus*, dir. Ridley Scott, Twentieth Century Fox, Dune Entertainment, 2012.

Chapter 2

1   Aristotle, *Poetics*, new edn, London: Penguin Classics, 1996.

2   Aeschylus, *The Oresteia* (trans. Robert Fagles), London: Penguin Classics, 1997.

3   Sophocles, *The Theban Plays* (trans. E. Watling), London: Penguin Classics, 1973.

4   Euripedes, *Medea and Other Plays* (trans. John Davie), London: Penguin Classics, 2003.

5   Sophocles, *The Theban Plays* (trans. E. Watling), London: Penguin Classics, 1973.

6   Abbott, H. Porter, *The Cambridge Introduction to Narrative*, 2nd edn, Cambridge: Cambridge University Press, 2008, p. 46.

7   Chatman, Seymour, *Coming to Terms: The Narrative of Fiction and Film*, Ithaca, NY: Cornell University Press, 1990.

8   *Blue Valentine*, dir. Derek Cianfrance, Incentive Filmed Entertainment, Silverwood Films, 2010.

9   *Memento*, dir. Christopher Nolan, Newmarket Capital Group, Team Todd, I Remember Productions, 2000.

10 Pinter, Harold, *Plays 4*, London: Faber and Faber, 2012.

11 Pinter, Harold, *Plays 3*, London: Faber and Faber, 1997.

12 Pinter, Harold, *Plays 2*, London: Faber and Faber, 1996.

13 McPherson, Conor, *The Weir*, new edn, London: Nick Hern Books, 2001.

14 Pinnock, Winsome, *Mules*, London: Faber and Faber, 1996.

15 Abbott, H. Porter, *The Cambridge Introduction to Narrative*, Cambridge: Cambridge University Press, 2008, p. 22.

16 *Mad Men*, created by Matthew Weiner, Lionsgate Television, Weiner Bros, AMC, 2007–.

17 *The Sopranos*, created by David Chase, HBO, Warner Bros, 1999–2007.

18 *Nil by Mouth*, dir. Gary Oldman, SE8 Group, EuropaCorp, 1997.

19 *Ratcatcher*, dir. Lynne Ramsay, Pathe Pictures International, BBC films, 1999.

20 *Kes*, dir. Ken Loach, Kestrel Films Ltd, Woodfall Productions, 1969.

21 *Shameless*, created by Paul Abbott, Company Pictures, Channel 4 Television, 2004–13.

Chapter 3

1   *Pulp Fiction*, dir. Quentin Tarantino, Miramax Films, 1994.

2   *Reservoir Dogs*, dir. Quentin Tarantino, Live Entertainment, Dog Eat Dog Productions, 1992.

3   McDonagh, Martin, *The Pilowman*, London: Faber and Faber, 2003.

4   *In Bruges*, dir. Martin McDonagh, Blueprint Pictures, Film 4, Focus Features, 2008.

5   *The Killing*, 'Forbrydelsen', created by Søren Sveistrup, DR, NRK, SVT, 2007–12.

6   *The Fall*, created by Allan Cubitt, Artists Studio, BBC Northern Ireland, 2013–.

7   Abrams, M. H., *A Glossary of Literary Terms*, 8th edn, Boston: Thomson Wadsworth, 2008, p. 332.

8   Seneca (trans. E. Watling), *Four Tragedies and Octavia*, new edn, London: Penguin Classics, 2005.

9   Ibid.

10 Seneca, *Apocolocyntosis* (trans. Allan Perley Ball), New York: Columbia University Press, 1902.

11 Seneca, *The Trojan Women* (trans. E. F. Watling), New York: Penguin Books, 1970.

12 Seneca, *Phaedra* (trans. E. F. Watling), New York: Penguin Books, 1970.

13 *Pulp Fiction*, dir. Quentin Tarantino, Miramax Films, 1994.

14 Seneca, *Phaedra* (trans. E. F. Watling), New York: Penguin Books, 1970.

Chapter 4

1 Kyd, Thomas, *The Spanish Tragedy*, revised edn, London: Methuen Drama, 2009.

2 *In the Bedroom*, dir. Todd Field, Good Machine, Standard Film Company, GreeneStreet Films, 2001.

3 *Get Carter*, dir. Mike Hodges, MGM British Studios, 1971.

4 *Oldboy*, dir. Chan-wook Park, Egg Films, Show East See, 2003.

5 *Straw Dogs*, dir. Sam Peckinpah, ABC Pictures, Talent Associates, 1971.

6 *Cape Fear*, dir J. Lee Thompson, Melville-Talbot Productions, 1962.

7 Shakespeare, *Hamlet*, Act 1, Scene 2, lines 133–134.

8 Dickens, Charles, *A Christmas Carol*, new edn, London: Penguin Classics, 2003.

9 *As Good as it Gets*, dir. James L. Brooks, Tristar Pictures, Gracie Films, 1997.

10 *About Schmidt*, dir. Alexander Payne, New Line Cinema, Avery Pix, 2002.

11 Shakespeare, *Hamlet*, Act 3, Scene 1, lines 83–88.

12 Sandra, Gilbert, *The Madwoman in the Attic, The Woman Writer and the Nineteenth Century Literary Imagination*, New Haven: Yale University Press, 2000.

13 Roland Barthes, 'Introduction to the Structural Analysis of Narratives' in Susan Sontag (ed.), *A Barthes Reader*, New York: Hill and Wang, 1974.

14 Beaumont, Francis, *Knight of the Burning Pestle*, new edn, London: Nick Hern Books, 2001.

15 Pirandello, Luigi, *Six Characters in Search of an Author and other Plays*, New York: Penguin Books, 1995.

16 Brecht, Bertolt, *The Caucasian Chalk Circle*, London: Penguin Classics, 2007.

17 Shakespeare, William, *Hamlet*, Act 1, Scene 2, lines 150–151.

18 Shakespeare, William, *Hamlet*, Act 4, Scene 5, lines 84–86.

19 *The Spanish Tragedy*, Act 2, Scene 1.

20 *The Spanish Tragedy*, Act 5, Scene 3.

21 Tillyard, E. M. W., *The Elizabethan World Picture*, London: Chatto and Windus, 1943, p.83.

22 Milton, *Paradise Lost*, Book IX, lines 1126–1130.

Chapter 5

1 *Django Unchained*, dir. Quentin Tarantino, The Weinstein Company, Columbia Pictures, 2012.

2 Webster, John, *The Duchess of Malfi*, new edn, London: Methuen Drama, 2003.

3 Middleton, Thomas and Rowley, William, *The Changeling*, new edn, London: Nick Hern Books, 2000.

4 Beaumont, Francis and Fletcher, John, *The Maid's Tragedy*.

5 Ford, John, *'Tis Pity She's a Whore*, new edn, London: Methuen Drama, 2003.

6 *Desperate Housewives*, created by Marc Cherry, Cherry Alley Productions, Cherry Productions, Touchstone Television, 2004–12.

7 *Sex and the City*, created by Darren Star, Darren Star Productions, HBO, 1998–2004.

8 *Girls*, created by Lena Dunham, Apatow Productions, HBO, 2012–.

9 Goldman, Emma, 'The Hypocrisy of Puritanism' in *Anarchism and Other Essays*, New York: Mother Earth Publishing Association, 1917.

10 'Beaumont, Francis and Fletcher, John, *The Maid's Tragedy*.' Manchester University Press (revised edition), 1999.

11 *Lost*, created by J. J. Abrams, Jeffrey Lieber and Damon Lindelof, ABC Studios, Touchstone Television, Bad Robot, 2004–10.

12 *Pulp Fiction*, dir. Quentin Tarantino, Miramax Films, 1994.

13 Beaumont, Francis and Fletcher, John, *The Maid's Tragedy*, Act 5, Scene 1.

14 *Buffy the Vampire Slayer*, created by Joss Whedon, Mutant Enemy, Kuzui Enterprises, Sandollar Television, 1997–2003.

15 *Once More with Feeling*, dir. Joss Whedon, Season 6, Episode 7 of *Buffy the Vampire Slayer,* Mutant Enemy, Kuzui Enterprises, Sandollar Television, first broadcast, 6 November 2001.

16 *The Silence of the Lambs*, dir. Jonathan Demme, Strong Heart/Demme Production, Orion Pictures Corporation, 1991.

17 Middleton, Thomas, *The Second Maiden's Tragedy*, in Martin Wiggins (ed.), *Four Jacobean Sex Tragedies*, Oxford: Oxford University Press, 1998.

Chapter 6

1 Menander, *Plays and Fragments*, London: Penguin Classics, 1987.

2 *Frasier*, created by David Angeli, Peter Casey and David Lee, Grub Street Productions, Paramount Television, 1993–2004.

3 Menander, *Plays and Fragments*, London: Penguin Classics, 1987.

4 *The Two Mrs Cranes*, dir. David Lee, Grub Street Productions, Paramount Television, Season 4, Episode 1, first broadcast 17 September 1996.

5 Abrams, M. H., *A Glossary of Literary Terms*, 8th edn, Boston: Thomson Wadsworth, 2005, p. 144.

6 *The Ski Lodge*, dir. David Lee, Grub Street Productions, Paramount Television, Season 5, Episode 14, first broadcast 24 February 1998.

7 *Fawlty Towers*, written by John Cleese and Connie Booth, BBC, 1975 and 1979.

8 *Gourmet Night,* dir. John Howard Davies, BBC, *Fawlty Towers*, Season 1, Episode 5, first broadcast 17 October 1975.

9 *Arrested Development*, created by Mitchell Hurwitz, Image Entertainment, 20th Century Fox, Hurwitz Company, 2003–13.

10 *New Girl*, created by Elizabeth Meriwether, Elizabeth Meriwether Pictures, American Nitwits, 2011–.

11 *Curb Your Enthusiasm*, created by Larry David, HBO films, Production Partners, 2000–.

12 Goldoni, Carlo, *A Servant to Two Masters* (trans. Lee Hall), London: Methuen Drama, 1999.

13 Bean, Richard, *One Man, Two Guvnors*, London: Oberon Books, 2011.

Chapter 7

1 Plautus, *The Pot of Gold and Other Plays*, London: Penguin Classics, 2004.

2 Plautus, *The Pot of Gold* (trans. E. F. Watling), London: Penguin Classics, 2004.

3 Ibid.

4 *Noises Off* by Michael Frayn has had numerous revivals in the UK and USA. *One Man, Two Guvnors* by Richard Bean is an updating of Goldoni's *The Servant to Two Masters*.

5 Miola, Robert S., 'Roman Comedy' in Alexander Leggatt (ed.), *The Cambridge Companion to Shakespearean Comedy*, Cambridge: Cambridge University Press, 2002, p.25.

6 Ibid, p.25.

7 Plautus, *The Pot of Gold and Other Plays*, London: Penguin Classics, 2004.

8 Rudlin, John, *Commedia dell'Arte: An Actor's Handbook*, London: Routledge, 1994, p.71.

9 Oreglia, Giacomo, *The Commedia dell'Arte* (trans. Lovett F. Edwards), London: Methuen, 1968.

10 Andrea Perrucci, *Dell'arte rappresentativa, premeditata e all'improvviso*, 1699.

11 The original series: *Scooby-Doo, Where Are You?*, written by Joe Ruby and Ken Spears, Hanna-Barbera Productions, 1969.

12 Fawlty Towers, written by John Cleese and Connie Booth, BBC, 1975 and 1979.

13 Fawlty Towers episodes: *Waldorf Salad* (1979), *The Kipper and The Corpse* (1979), and *Gourmet Night* (1975).

14 *Friends*, created by David Crane and Martha Kauffman, Warner Bros. Television, Bright/Kauffman/Crane Productions, 1994–2004.

15 Da Ali G. Show, created by Sacha Baron Cohen, Talkback Productions, 2000–3.

16 Gibson, Janine, 'Comics find Ali G is an alibi for racism', *The Guardian*, 11 January 2000.

17 *The Dictator*, dir. Larry Charles, written by Sacha Baron Cohen, Alec Burg, David Mandel and Jeff Schaffer, Paramount Pictures and Four by Two Films, 2012.

18 Wilde, Oscar, *The Importance of Being Earnest and Other Plays*, Oxford: Oxford English Drama, 2008.

19 Aristotle, *The Poetics*, II, 2319 (1449a).

20 Banks-Smith, Nancy, 'Last Night's Television', *The Guardian*, 25 October 2005.

Chapter 8

1 Ellen, Barbara, 'The Name's Norton. Graham Norton', *The Observer*, 18 November 2007.

2 Fisher, Helen, *The brain in love*, TED talk, July 2008, www.ted.com

3 *Tootsie*, dir. Sydney Pollack, Columbia Pictures, Mirage Enterprises, 1982.

4 *Some Like it Hot*, dir. Billy Wilder, Ashton Productions, Mirisch Corporation, 1959.

5 Shakespeare, *Twelfth Night*, Act 1, Scene 4.

6 Ibid., Act 2, Scene 4.

7 *Sabrina*, dir. Billy Wilder, Paramount Pictures, 1954.

8 *Four Weddings and a Funeral*, dir. Mike Newell, Polygram Filmed Entertainment, Channel Four Films, Working Title Films, 1994.

9 *Crazy, Stupid, Love*, dir. Glenn Ficarra and John Requa, Carousel Productions, 2011.

10 Rostand, Edmond, *Cyrano de Bergerac*, London: Penguin Classics, 2006.

11 Interesting to note the two Hollywood comedies *Friends with Benefits* (2011) and *No Strings Attached* (2011), which were released more or less at the same time. Both involved sexual intimacy between the characters before they had acknowledged that they had fallen in love. A reordering of the courtship process is needed.

12 *Crazy, Stupid, Love*, dir. Glenn Ficarra and John Requa, Carousel Productions, 2011.

13 Fisher, Helen, *Why we love, why we cheat*, TED talk, September 2006, www.ted.com

14 Book of Genesis 2:24 (*King James Bible*).

15 *When Harry Met Sally*, dir. Rob Reiner, Castle Rock Entertainment, 1989.

16 *Sleepless in Seattle*, dir. Nora Ephron, TriStar Pictures, 1993.

Chapter 9

1 *Mean Girls*, dir. Mark Waters, Paramount Pictures, M.G. Films, Broadway Video, 2004.

2 *Clueless*, dir. Amy Heckerling, Paramount Pictures, 1995.

3 *Legally Blonde*, Robert Luketic, MGM, Marc Platt Productions, 2001.

4 Nietzsche, Friedrich, (trans. Marion Faber) *Beyond Good and Evil*, Oxford Paperbacks, 2008, p.156.

5 Callow, Simon, *Acting in Restoration Comedy*, New York: Applause Theatre Books, 1991.

6 *Parks and Recreation*, created by Greg Daniels, Deedle-Dee Productions, 3 Arts Entertainment, Universal Media Studios, 2009–.

7 *30 Rock*, created by Tina Fey, Broadway Video, Little Stranger, NBC Studios, 2006–13.

8 *Community*, created by Dan Harmon, Krasnoff Foster Productions, Harmonious Claptrap, Russo Brothers, 2009–.

9 Wycherley, William, *The Country Wife*, new edn, London: Methuen Drama, 2003.

10 Ibid, Act 2, Scene 1, lines 53–59.

11 *The Office*, created by Ricky Gervais, BBC, 2001–3.

12 Callow, Simon, *Acting in Restoration Comedy*, New York: Applause Theatre Books, 1991, p.52.

13 Wycherley, William, *The Country Wife*, Act 1, Scene 1.

14 Ibid, Act 1, Scene 1.

15 Vanbrugh, John, *The Relapse*, Act 2, Scene 1.

16 *Behind the Candelabra*, dir. Steven Soderbergh, HBO films, 2013.

17 *Knowing Me, Knowing You with Alan Partridge*, created by Steve Coogan, Armando Iannucci and Patrick Marber, Talkback Productions, 1994–5.

18 Abrams, M. H., *A Glossary of Literary Terms*, New York: The Sauders Press, 1912, p.197.

19 Ibid, p.197.

20 Congreve, William, *The Way of the World*, 3rd edn, London: Methuen Drama, 2002.

21 *Friends*, created by David Crane and Marta Kauffman, Warner Bros Television, Bright/Kauffman/Crane Productions, 1994–2004.

22 *New Girl*, created by Elizabeth Meriwether, Elizabeth Meriwether Pictures, American Nitwits, Chernin Entertainment, 2011–.

23 Goldsmith, Oliver, *Comparison between Sentimental and Laughing Comedy*, 1773.

Chapter 10

1 Letter to Suvorin, 4 May 1889.

2 Turgenev, Ivan, *A Month in the Country* (trans. Emlyn Williams), New York: Samuel French, 2009.

3 Chekhov, Anton, *Plays* (trans. Peter Carson), London: Penguin Classics, 2002.

4 Butterworth, Jez, *Jerusalem*, London: Nick Hern Books, 2009.

5 Raine, Nina, *Tribes*, London: Nick Hern Books, 2010.

6 McCraney, Tarrell Alvin, *Choir Boy*, London: Faber and Faber, 2012.

7 *The Ice Storm*, dir. Ang Lee, Fox Searchlight Pictures, Good Machine, Canal + , 1997.

8 *The Big Chill*, dir. Lawrence Kasdan, Columbia Pictures Corporation, Carson Pictures, 1983.

9 *The Royal Tenenbaums*, dir. Wes Anderson, Touchstone Pictures, American Empirical Pictures, 2001.

10 *Margot at the Wedding*, dir. Noah Baumbach, Scott Rudin Productions, 2007.

11 Pitcher, Harvey, 'The Checkhov Play' in Rene Wellek and Nona D. Wellek (eds), *Chekhov, New Perspectives*, New Jersey: Prentice-Hall, 1984.

12 Chekhov, Anton, *Plays* (trans. Peter Carson), London: Penguin Classics, 2002.

13 Ibid.

14 Forster, E. M. *Aspects of the Novel*, London: Penguin Classics (New Edition), 2005.

15 Dickens, Charles, *David Copperfield*, Wordsworth Classics, 1992.

16 Wade, Laura, *Posh*, Oberon Modern Plays, 2010.

17 *Hannah and Her Sisters*, dir. Woody Allen, Orion Pictures Corporation, Jack Rollins and Charles H. Joffe Productions, 1986.

18 Chekhov, Anton, *Plays* (trans. Peter Carson), London: Penguin Classics, 2002.

19 *Gavin and Stacey*, created by James Corden and Ruth Jones, Baby Cow Productions, 2007–9.

20 *Girls*, created by Lena Dunham, Apatow Productions, 2012–.

21 Shchukin, S., *Memoirs,* 1911.

Chapter 11

1 *The Wizard of Oz*, dir. Victor Fleming, MGM, 1939.

2 Tolkein, J. R. R., *The Lord of the Rings*, new edn, London: HarperCollings, 2007.

3 *Indiana Jones and the Temple of Doom*, dir. Steven Spielberg, Paramount Pictures, Lucasfilm, 1984.

4 *Star Wars: Episode IV – A New Hope*, dir. George Lucas, Lucasfilm, Twentieth Century Fox Film, 1977.

5 Rowling, J. K., *Harry Potter and the Philosopher's Stone*, London: Bloomsbury Publishing, 2001.

6 Campbell, Joseph, *The Hero with A Thousand Faces*, new edn, San Francisco: New World Library, 2012.

7 Vogler, Christopher, *The Writer's Journey*, 3rd edn, Studio City, California: Michael Wiese Production, 2007.

8 Yorke, John, *Into the Woods*, London: Particular Books, 2013.

9 von Eschenbach, Wolfram, *Parzival* (trans. A. Hatto), London: Penguin Classics, 1980.

10 von Strassburg, Gottfried, *Tristan* (trans. A. Hatto), London: Penguin Classics, 1974.

11 *Sir Gawain and the Green Knight* (in a version by Simon Armitage), London: Faber and Faber, 2009.

12 Abrams, M. H. *A Glossary of literary Terms* (eighth edition), Boston: Thomson Wordsworth, 2005, p.127.

13 *Cars*, dir. John Lasseter and Joe Ranft, Walt Disney Pictures, Pixar Animation Studios, 2006.

14 *Finding Nemo*, dir. Andrew Stanton and Lee Unkrich, Walt Disney Pictures, Pixar Animation Studios, 2003.

15 *WALL-E*, dir. Andrew Stanton, Walt Disney Pictures, Pixar Animation Studios, 2008.

16 Monsters, Inc., dir. Pete Docter, David Silverman and Lee Unkrich, Walt Disney Pictures, Pixar Animation Studios, 2001.

17 Shakespeare, *As You Like it*, Act 2, Scene 1, lines 15–18.

18 Shakespeare, *The Tempest*, Act 5, Scene 1.

19 *Hart of Dixie*, created by Leila Gerstein, Fake Empire, CBS Television Studios, Warner Bros. Television, 2011–.

Appendix 1

1 *Nosferatu*, dir. F. W. Murnau, Prana Film GMBH, 1922.

2 *The Simpsons*, created by Matt Groening, Gracie Films, 20th Century Fox, 1989–.

3 *The Cabin in the Woods*, dir. Drew Goddard, Lionsgate, Mutant Enemy, 2012.

4 *Scream*, dir. Wes Craven, Dimension Films, Woods Entertainment, 1996.

5 Koltes, Bernard-Marie, *Roberto Zucco*, Methuen Drama, 1997.

6 *Dawson's Creek*, created by Kevin Williamson, Outerbank Entertainment, Columbia TriStar Television, 1998–2003.

7 *90210*, created by Jeff Judah, Gabe Sachs, Darren Star and Rob Thomas, Sachs/Judah Productions, CBS Productions, CBS Television Studios, 2008–13.

8 *The O.C.*, created by Josh Schwartz, Wonderland Sound and Vision, Warner Bros. Television, 2003–7.

Appendix 2

1 Campbell, Joseph, *The Hero with a Thousand Faces*, 3rd edn, San Franchiso: New World Library, 2012.

2 Field, Syd, *Screenplay: The Foundations of Screenwriting*, Random House: Bantam Dell, 1979.

3 McKee, Robert, *Story*, London: Methuen, 1997.

4 Vogler, Christopher, *The Writer's Journey*, revised edn, London: Pan Macmillan, 1999.

5 Snyder, Blake, *Save the Cat!* Michael Wiese Productions, 2005.

6 Booker, Christopher, *The Seven Basic Plots: Why We Tell Stories*, New York: Continuum International Publishing, 2005.

7 Yorke, John, *Into the Woods: A Five Act Journey into Story*, London: Particular Books, 2013.

8 Greig, Noël, *Playwriting A Practical Guide*, London: Routledge, 2005.

9 Edgar, David, *How Plays Work*, London: Nick Hern Books, 2009.

10 Abbott, H. Porter, *The Cambridge Introduction to Narrative*, Cambridge: Cambridge University Press, 2008.